Apps for Learning

40 Best iPad/iPod Touch/iPhone Apps
for High School Classrooms

21st Century Fluency Project

Andrew Churches

Andrew Churches is a teacher and ICT enthusiast. He teaches at Kristin School on Auckland's North Shore, a school with a mobile computing program that sees students with personal mobile devices and laptops. He is an edublogger, wiki author, and innovator. In 2008, Andrew's wiki, Educational Origami, was nominated for the Edublogs Best Wiki awards. He contributes to a number of web sites and blogs including Techlearning, Spectrum Education magazine, and the Committed Sardine Blog. Andrew believes that to prepare our students for the future we must prepare them for change and teach them to question, think, adapt, and modify.

Harry Dickens

Harry Dickens is the technology director for the Arkansas Public School Resource Center. Prior to his position at the center, Harry was a classroom teacher in Texarkana and El Dorado, Arkansas. He left the classroom to become the instructional technology director for the Texarkana School District. Harry teaches professional development classes on infusing technology into instruction throughout Arkansas, as well as at national conferences. He is a member of the core Technology Infused Education (TIE) team, a technology group of more than 100 instructional technology trainers in Arkansas. Harry is also a member of the Technology Information Center for Administrative Leadership (TICAL), which is a cadre of administrators that contributes new technology resources and provides orientation and training sessions throughout the state. He is currently serving on the Arkansas State technology planning committee and is chairing the teaching and learning subcommittee. Harry believes that receiving education content extends beyond district or state boundaries. He also believes we must embrace mobile technologies as a teaching tool, as well as a delivery mechanism for relevant content for classrooms. Harry has a wife named Quita and two young sons, Harrison and Jordan.

21st Century Fluency Project

co-published with

CORWIN
A SAGE Company

For information:
21st Century Fluency Project Inc.
1890 Grant St.
Vancouver BC Canada V5L 2Y8

www.fluency21.com

ISBN-13:978-1463612856
ISBN-10:1463612850

Acquisitions Editor: Debra Stollenwerk
Editorial, Production, and Indexing: Abella Publishing Services, LLC
Design/Typesetting: Ross Crockett
Cover Designer: Lee Crockett

Disclaimer
Every attempt has been made to contact known copyright holders included in this work. Any errors are unintended and should be brought to the attention of the publisher for corrections in subsequent printings.

Contents

Section 3: Specialty Apps

21st Century Fluency Project

The 21st Century Fluency Project is about moving vision into practice through the process of investigating the impact of technology on our society and our children over the last few decades, learning how we in education must evolve, and, finally, committing to changes at the classroom level.

Living on the Future Edge is the first book in our 21st Century Fluency Series. We face a world on the move, and education needs to react. A series of six books, as well as related supporting materials, has been developed in order to answer five essential questions that teachers will ask when considering how educators and education must respond to the profound developments that are being experienced in the world at large.

Why Do I Have to Change?

Living on the Future Edge

Windows on Tomorrow

In this book, we discuss the power of paradigm to shape our thinking, the pressure that technological development is putting on our paradigm for teaching and learning, six exponential trends in technological development that we can't ignore, what these trends mean for education, new skills for students, new roles for teachers, and scenarios of education in the future.

Understanding the Digital Generation

Teaching and Learning in the New Digital Landscape

This book examines the effects that digital bombardment from constant exposure to electronic media has on kids in the new digital landscape and considers the profound implications this holds for the future of education. What does the latest neuroscientific and psychological research tell us about the role of intense and frequent experiences on the brain, particularly the young and impressionable brain?

Based on the research, what inferences can we make about kids' digital experiences and how these experiences are rewiring and reshaping their cognitive processes? More important, what are the implications for teaching, learning, and assessment in the new digital landscape?

How can we reconcile these new developments with current instructional practices, particularly in a climate of standards and accountability driven by high-stakes testing for all? What strategies can we use to appeal to the learning preferences and communication needs of digital learners while at the same time honoring our traditional assumptions and practices related to teaching, learning, and assessment?

Where Do I Start?

The Digital Diet

Today's Digital Tools in Small Bytes

This book offers bite-sized, progressively challenging projects to introduce the reader to the digital landscape of today. This is the world of our children and students. *The Digital Diet* will help readers shed pounds of assumptions and boost their digital metabolism to help keep pace with these kids by learning to use some simple yet powerful digital tools.

What Would This Teaching Look Like in My Classroom?

Literacy Is Not Enough

21st Century Fluencies for the Digital Age

It is no longer enough that we educate only to the standards of the traditional literacies. To be competent and capable in the 21st century requires a completely different set of skills—the 21st-century fluencies—that are identified and explained in detail in this book. The balance of the book introduces our framework for integrating these fluencies in our traditional curriculum.

21st Century Fluency Kits

These kits are subject- and grade-specific publications designed to integrate the teaching of 21st-century fluencies into today's curriculum and classroom. Included are detailed learning scenarios, resources, rubrics, and lesson plans with suggestions for high-tech, low-tech, or no-tech implementation. Also identified is the traditional content covered, as well as the standards and 21st-century fluencies each project covers.

Apps for Learning

40 Best iPad/iPod Touch/iPhone Apps

In the classroom of the 21st century, the power of mobility has begun to play a significant role in the learning experiences of our students. The ubiquitous digital devices they use so frequently and unconsciously can be harnessed as powerful tools for learning, creativity, and discovery. And, as the saying goes, "there's an app for that."

This remarkable and revealing three-book series on the best choices for learning apps in the classroom covers mobility apps categories for utilities, general classroom applications, and also specialty apps designed with unique learning tools that students can utilize both in class and on the go. Each book is devoted to a specific grade level—one each for elementary school, middle school, and high school.

The *Apps for Learning* books will show how both you and your students can get the most out of our versatile mobile technology and turn the classroom into a personal digital adventure in learning.

The 21st Century Fluency Project Web Site

www.fluency21.com

Our web site contains supplemental material that provides support for classroom teachers who are implementing 21st-century teaching. The site lets teachers access pre-made lesson plans that teach traditional content along with 21st-century fluencies. The site also provides teachers with a blank template for designing their own lessons for teaching 21st-century fluencies. There are also other shared resources and a forum for additional collaboration and support.

How Can We Design Effective Schools for the 21st Century?

Teaching the Digital Generation

No More Cookie Cutter-High Schools

The world has changed. Young people have changed. But the same underlying assumptions about teachers, students, and instruction that have guided high school design for a hundred years continue to shape the way high schools are designed today. In fact, so much is assumed about the way a high school should look, that new schools are created from a long-established template without question. Strip away the skylights, the fancy foyers, and the high-tech PA systems, and new schools being constructed today look pretty much the way they did when most adults went to school.

This is a mismatch with reality. We need new designs that incorporate what we have learned about young people and how they learn best. This book outlines a new process for designing high schools and provides descriptions of several new models for how schools can be configured to better support learning.

Preface

Everyone's heard Apple's catchphrase: "There's an app for that." But what does this mean to educators? The App Store contains an amazing number of apps—over 400,000—and determining which will be useful in your classroom could be a daunting task. This book contains a collection of the apps we have used to plan lessons, aid in professional development sessions, and help students become more productive in the classroom, and we hope you'll find it useful in selecting the ones that are right for you and your students.

It is not surprising that the iPad and iPod Touch have an immense impact on education training opportunities. There is a vast library of applications available for iPads and iPod Touches through iTunes that have the potential to change the way we deliver content in the classroom and the way our students consume it. One of the biggest trends in technology is the flexibility to be mobile. The iPad and iPod Touch are moving us quickly toward this way of teaching and learning. They empower students to accomplish learning when and where it is convenient or practical for them to do so. No longer will education be confined to school buildings. It will take place in parks, on buses, on boats, in museums, on football fields, at the ocean shore, and so on. Learning will take place almost anywhere students have a teachable moment, which makes learning more relevant. Using the apps on the iPad and iPod Touch, students and teachers have the ability to create and contribute content from anywhere at any time.

This book has several goals. One is to give educators an overview of the best apps for iPad and iPod Touch and how they can fit into their classroom instruction and productivity. Second, this book will, we hope, challenge teachers to think differently about their classrooms and the potential of incorporating iPad and iPod Touch apps into their lessons to engage students. Many of the apps allow the walls of the classroom to come down because of their "web ability"—they allow students to access web content anywhere.

There will always be naysayers who think this is just a fad. However, sales of more than 10 million mobile devices and more than 10 billion apps downloaded from the iTunes store is more than a fad. Every district, administrator, and teacher needs to be on board! There will be issues with such a shift from what we once did to these new mobile devices and apps that put our children on the Internet to collaborate, create, and connect. The world is not perfect, and issues that arise will need to be turned into teachable moments.

The iPad and iPod Touch apps, as well as the devices themselves, are constantly changing. They are evolving into tools that allow access to many ways of understanding content. They are the perfect companion for the student who would like to use video to show understanding or audio for his or her explanation of a complex problem or a teacher creating content that can be played back in the car, on the school bus, or in the cafeteria on a device that students are more apt to use. Apple has sold more than 15 million iPads, and iPad 2 sales have not slowed down. These and other mobile devices are entering the classroom as the device of choice. Many states are requiring digital content and a way to present that content. Mobile devices are changing the way we teach and learn quickly. Enjoy the change!

Introduction

On January 22, 2011, Apple announced its 10 billionth application had been downloaded from the App Store. For the 160 million iPod Touch, iPhone, and iPad users worldwide, the App Store offers more than 400,000 apps, with 60,000 specifically developed for the iPad (http://www.apple.com/pr/library/2011/01/22appstore.html).

The iPad, iPhone, and iPod Touch have revolutionized the concept of a media player, cell phone, and personal computing device, and it's not at all surprising that these devices have made their way into the classroom.

Initially treated with a degree of fear and skepticism, these tools have the potential to change the face of teaching and learning. No longer are they a single-purpose device like the early cellular or mobile phone, which allowed users to talk to or text a colleague. They are much more sophisticated than devices that only a few short years ago could only provide simple reminders and calendars, a camera, and a few games. The tools we have today are highly functional and powerful computers capable of not only consuming, but also creating.

Some commentators have said devices such as the iPad are primarily for consumption in that they are designed to access and view or play media—and that may be the case for many users who have these devices at home. Even so, as a device for consumption, the "i" devices are media playing, communication and collaboration enabling, web surfing, book reading tools with immense potential.

In a classroom setting, however, they move from a device for consumption to a device for production. While it is true that the ability to program and develop software on them is very limited, the application of programming in schools is usually limited to specialist subject areas. For the average student, this lack is insignificant since the "i" devices are overflowing with tools for creative expression, collaboration, and communication. Their portability, ease of use, and clean design make them appealing. Add to this their customization ability, the simplicity of adding further tools, and their potential for connectivity and accessibility and it is easy to see why these devices are tools that can be used in the classroom, across the curriculum, and spanning all age ranges.

The diversity of applications available at low or no cost from the App Store allows users to develop documents, spreadsheets, and presentations; edit videos; create and record podcasts and music; create, edit, and manipulate graphics and images; produce mind maps, charts, comics, cartoons, and picture books; publish tweets, blogs, and wikis; surf the Internet; read and send emails; and audio conference one to one or one to many—and these are just a few of the creative and productive elements the devices are capable of.

From our experience with the range of students we teach and how our own children use these devices, we have seen even the youngest children—pre-kindergartners who are essentially illiterate—be able to navigate and manipulate the tools. The finger-driven interface is a natural extension for young and old—it's quick to learn, intuitive, and simple. One of the earliest motor skills to develop in children is the ability to point, and with this ability to point they are easily able to manipulate these devices.

As educators, we accept that the world our students graduate into is going to be a digital one. Let's face it, the world is experiencing exponential change, and clearly this means we must prepare students for the dynamically new environment they will face on graduation.

For most of our graduates, the last meaningful thing they will do with a pen is to write their last examination. We have witnessed first computers in labs, then computers in classrooms, and most recently laptop programs, with administrators and teachers recognizing that computers are not about just-in-case learning, but more about just-in-time capturing of the teachable moment. We have seen the change from these computer technologies being rare and expensive to what they are today—accessible, ubiquitous, and affordable. Our students bring powerful computers with Internet connectivity, real-time communication tools, cameras, audio recorders, media players, and productivity tools with them into the classroom.

The "i" devices are powerful, portable, affordable, and accessible—and they provide a real alternative to having class sets of computers, pods of laptops, and laboratories full of desktops. While these "traditional" tools still have a place in our schools, the "i" devices are a cost-efficient alternative.

Today, the world is our classroom. While most school administrators don't mind the pod of laptops moving between classes, they would be concerned with them moving beyond the boundaries of the buildings. And it is obviously impossible to take the computer lab into the field. However, "i" devices provide a solution for the use of technology beyond the confines of the four walls of our classrooms. Portable, robust, and connected, these devices open huge possibilities for education outside of school. The range of applications and ease of connection means that students can work in situ, making their learning experience immediate and, therefore, far more relevant.

What Are Apps for Learning?

Apps for Learning is a snapshot of some of the best and most appropriate applications for the iPad, iPod Touch, and iPhone for use in the classroom. Written by classroom practitioners for classroom practitioners, it ties together teaching experiences using these tools from across curriculum areas and throughout grade levels. The tools detailed in this book are ones with which we have had personal and professional experience, and they have been selected because of their practicality and applicability for use in the classroom.

For each app, we have given you the basics and the classroom application. The basics cover cost, application type, curriculum area (where applicable), and basic functions and features. The classroom application shows how we have applied the tool to our teaching and learning practice. Because of the limitations of space, these are detailed and specific to one or two examples, but in most cases we have had many, many more applications for them in our classrooms. We have attempted to show a use for them that will spark you to apply these tools in your practice and to engage your creativity and passion for teaching to adapt these starters into a myriad of different forms and uses.

How to Use This Book

The best place to start is in the area you are passionate about. Whether it is language arts, mathematics, the sciences, media, or physical education, there are applications that will suit you. Read the description and classroom use, and install the application. Many of the tools we have suggested are free or are available in both low/no-cost and premium forms.

We know the best way to learn anything about an application is to play with it. Be sure to investigate the different features of these apps and consider how you could use them personally, in your classroom and beyond.

The apps selected are ones that can be used individually, as well as having application to class sets of devices. Whether it is Apple's iWorks Pages (for word processing), iThoughtsHD (a "mind-mapping" tool), Adobe Photoshop PS Express (for enhancing your photos), or Comic Touch (a graphics application), these tools will enhance your teaching and your students' learning.

As with all things technology-related, the world of apps is constantly changing. It's very important to remember that new and exciting apps with incredible learning potential are being created every day. Just as quickly, some apps are phasing out to make way for the new and improved. Please be aware that the apps profiled in the following pages are indicative of what was available at the time this book was printed. Although rare, you may find that one or two of the apps listed are no longer available. We strongly suggest that you keep a close eye on learning apps development to pinpoint others that may suit your needs above and beyond what this series offers. It's a big apps world out there, and it's waiting for you to go and explore it.

Have fun, play, and learn!

Apps at a Glance

Quick Reference Chart

Utility Apps

App Name	Description	Subject Area	Available for	Cost (iPad/iPod)
Atomic Web Browser	Customized Web Browser	All	iPad/iPod Touch/ iPhone	$0.99/Free
Box.net	Online Storage	All	iPad/iPod Touch/ iPhone	Free
GoodReader	File Manager/ Distribution	All	iPad	$4.99
Print n Share	Printing/Utility	All	iPad/iPod Touch/ iPhone	$8.99/$6.99

General Apps

App Name	Description	Subject Area	Available for	Cost (iPad/iPod)
Adobe Photoshop PS Express	Image Editor	All	iPad/iPod Touch/ iPhone	Free
Dragon Dictation	Speech-to-Text	All	iPad/iPod Touch/ iPhone	Free
eClicker Host/ eClicker	Personal Response System	All	iPad/iPod Touch/ iPhone	$9.99
Evernote	Task Organizer	All	iPad/iPod Touch/ iPhone	Free (Basic)
GarageBand	Music Creator	Performing Arts	iPad/iPod Touch/ iPhone	$4.99
Google Earth	Geographical Information	Geography	iPad/iPod Touch/ iPhone	Free
iBooks	Ebook Downloads	All	iPad/iPod Touch/ iPhone	Free
iMovie	Movie Editor	All	iPad/iPod Touch/ iPhone	$4.99
iThoughts HD	Mind Mapping	All	iPad	$9.99
iTranslate/ iTranslate Plus	Translator	Language Studies	iPad/iPod Touch/ iPhone	Free (Basic)/ $1.99 (Plus)
Keynote	Presentation Tool	All	iPad/iPod Touch/ iPhone	$9.99

General Apps (cont'd)

App Name	Description	Subject Area	Available for	Cost (iPad/iPod)
Keynote Remote	Remote Control for Keynote	All	iPad/iPod Touch/ iPhone	$0.99
Lynkee 2 QR Barcode Reader	Barcode Reader	All	iPad/iPod Touch/ iPhone	Free
Note Taker HD	Note taking App	All	iPad	$4.99
Numbers	Data Organizer/ Spreadsheets	All	iPad/iPod Touch/ iPhone	$9.99
Pages	Word Processor	All	iPad/iPod Touch/ iPhone	$9.99
Skype	Video Conferencing	All	iPad/iPod Touch/ iPhone	Free
TED	Presentation Archives	All	iPad	Free
Teleprompt+	Teleprompter	All	iPad	$14.99
Whiteboard HD	Interactive Whiteboard	All	iPad	$4.99
Wikihood/ Wikihood Plus	Wikipedia Extension	History/ U.S. History	iPad/iPod Touch/ iPhone	$6.99/Free

Specialty Apps

App Name	Description	Subject Area	Available for	Cost (iPad/iPod)
Algebra Touch	Algebra Special App	Math	iPad/iPod Touch/ iPhone	$1.99
Comic Touch/ Comic Touch Lite	Comic Creator	All	iPad/iPod Touch/ iPhone	$2.99/Free
EMD PTE	Interactive Periodic Table	Science	iPad/iPod Touch/ iPhone	Free
Frog Dissection	Dissection Simulator	Science	iPad	$3.99
gFlashPro	Flashcards and Test	All	iPad/iPod Touch/ iPhone	$3.99
iMathematics	Math Resources	Math	iPad/iPod Touch/ iPhone	Free
Manual for the U.S.A.	Historical Archive	U.S. History/ Social Studies	iPad/iPod Touch/ iPhone	$2.99

Specialty Apps (cont'd)

App Name	Description	Subject Area	Available for	Cost (iPad/iPod)
NASA App HD	NASA Special App	Science/ Social Studies	iPad/iPod Touch/ iPhone	Free
Play2Learn	Vocabulary Teaching Tool	Language Arts	iPad/iPod Touch/ iPhone	$1.99
Rory's Story Cubes	Story Generator	English/ Drama	iPad/iPod Touch/ iPhone	$1.99
Schmoop	Literary Learning Guide	Language Arts	iPad/iPod Touch/ iPhone	$1.99
Stack the States/ Countries	Geography Puzzle Game	Social Science/ History	iPad/iPod Touch/ iPhone	$0.99/Free
StoryKit	Electronic Storybook	All	iPad/iPod Touch/ iPhone	Free
VideoScience	Science Video Archive	Science	iPad/iPod Touch/ iPhone	$0.99
World Factbook	World Information Archive	Geography/ Reference	iPad/iPod Touch/ iPhone	$0.99

Section 1

Utility APPS

Atomic Web Browser

about the app

App name: Atomic Web Browser / Atomic Web Browser Lite
Subject areas: All
Available for: iPad / iPhone / iPod Touch
Cost: $0.99 for iPad / Free for iPhone and iPod Touch
Requirements: Requires iOS 3.0 or later. Internet connection needed to view web pages.
iTunes URL: http://itunes.apple.com/us/app/atomic-web-browser-browse/id347929410?mt=8
Developer web site: http://atomicwebbrowser.com/
Internet required: Yes

What Is Atomic Web Browser?

Atomic Web Browser is a customizable, full-screen web browser with VGA out capabilities for the first generation iPad. The second generation iPad, iPad 2, has full-screen sharing that allows the user to share the application on an external screen, monitor, projector, or television. An adapter is required to connect to the external device. This optimized browser has a variety of options, allowing you to add advanced privacy control, use ad blocker, customize searches, and have the Web recognize the app as a different browser, such as Internet Explorer or Firefox. With Atomic Web Browser, students and teachers can customize their browsing experience. Many of the above mentioned options can be seen in Figure 1 and Figure 2.

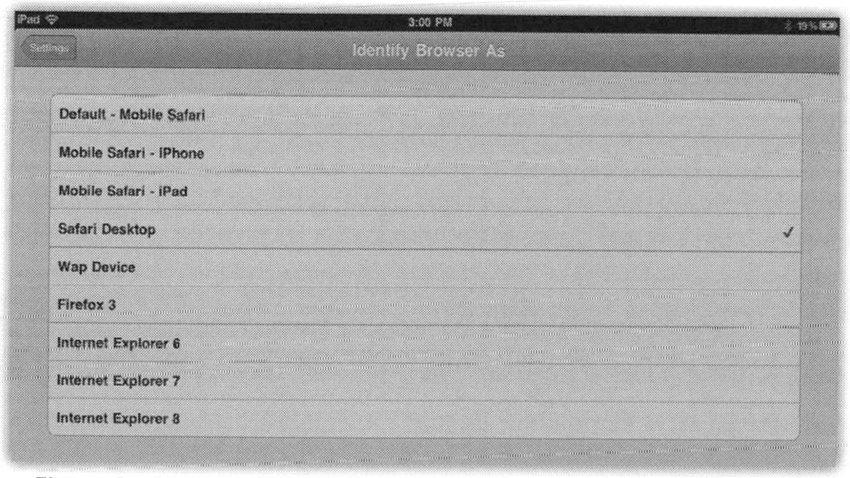

Figure 1—*Browser options 1*

Features

- *Download* – Images or files can be downloaded in the background; multiple downloads can run at the same time

- *Adblock* – Blocks most ad banners through URL filters

- *Tabs* – Users can choose between desktop-style tabs or list view

- *Identify As* – Spoofs web sites into thinking the browser is from a desktop computer using Safari; Firefox 3; Internet Explorer 6, 7, or 8; or a WAP (wireless access protocol) device

- *Video Out* – Video out to display web pages on TVs or projectors

- *File Transfer* – Dropbox, iTunes Document Sharing, email

- *File Management* – Save documents in the browser and create folders for better file management

- *MultiTouch Gestures* – Five multitouch gestures are supported that allow users to simultaneously register positions of input on the screen using one, two, or three fingers

- *User Agent Switcher*

- *Passcode Lock* – When enabled, requires a passcode to use

- *Facebook/Twitter integration through "quick buttons"*

- *Save Page* – Saves pages for off-line viewing

How Does Atomic Web Browser Work?

This app has features that closely resemble a desktop web browser. In Figure 2, users can see that Atomic Web Browser has full-screen mode, which limits the distractions on a web page. This can be enabled with the icon in the upper right corner of the browser.

Figure 2—*Browser options 2*

With Atomic Web Browser, you can view pages in tabs and have multiple downloads happening in the background. The web browser allows you to bookmark, email, and print browsed pages quickly. You also can share pages to a social network, such as Twitter or Facebook, or send pages by email. These options, seen in Figure 3, are at the bottom of the browser window or can be found by clicking on the plus sign (+) at the top of the browser.

Figure 3—*Sharing options*

The built-in Safari browser for Apple's iOS device can feel rather limited, especially when compared with the desktop version of Safari. However, limitations aren't really a problem with Atomic Web Browser because its settings are what sets it apart from other browsers. It provides general settings, user interface settings, action settings, and other controls.

General settings include privacy options, allowing you to set a password to use the web browser. Atomic Web Browser has nine search engines included, although more can be added. Likewise, any of the nine can be deleted.

The Identify Browser option is very useful when you have sites that display better in different browsers. There are several choices including mobile versions of Safari, Firefox, and Internet Explorer 6, 7, and 8. The user interface includes color themes, as well as multitask and gesture options.

The full-screen options make this app remarkable. In addition to the option of a tab bar, there are several full-screen options (shown in Figure 4 below) that will allow you to do several actions without going into the settings of the app. The buttons that are added to the bottom of the browser help with multitasking. Other controls allow for images to display on web pages or VGA out for use with a projector or television, for those using the first generation iPad.

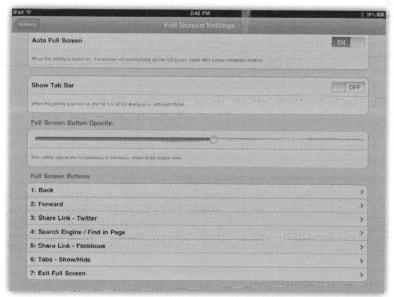

Figure 4—*Full-screen options*

How Can Atomic Web Browser Be Used in the Classroom?

The optimized browser allows it to be customized to fit the needs of the teachers and students. The browser has the familiar "look" of a desktop and offers users the ability to view web pages in tabs. Atomic Web Browser requires an Internet connection for viewing live web pages. Downloaded pages can be viewed off-line.

Atomic Web Browser has a download manager for files downloaded from the Internet. Files downloaded in the browser can be sent to "open in applications." Others can be emailed as long as the files are 15 megabytes or less. Files can be viewed in the browser if they are sent to Dropbox online storage, emailed, or opened in another application. The Atomic Web Browser can be a file manager and allow students and teachers to save files in the browser or to create folders for better file management. Users can connect to a projector using a VGA adapter.

Using iTunes Steps

- Open iTunes while your iPad is connected to a computer.
- On the iPad, click on apps at the bottom.
- Using file sharing, you can add files to Atomic Web.
- The file will appear and can be used by the browser off-line.
- Follow the same steps to download the MP3 file. (Remember to add the .mp3 extension to the file name.) Then, you can open two tabs to show one for the PDF and one for the MP3.

Advanced Uses

An advanced use of Atomic Web Browser could be combining the text of complex math problems with an audio file explaining the steps to solve them. This could be teacher- or student-created files from a web site. Another classroom use could be to listen to famous speeches from historical figures such as President John F. Kennedy and Dr. Martin L. King, Jr.

Lit2Go (Figure 5) is a free collection of stories and poems in MP3 format. The site also has text of the audio file. With Atomic Web Browser, you can download the text and the audio files list, save them, and open both in different tabs. You can also listen and read.

Figure 5—Lit2Go

Using the iPad

- Go to http://etc.usf.edu/lit2go/index.htm.

- You can browse by author, title, reading level (Flesch-Kincaid), or subject matter.

- Choose a title and click on Download PDF.

- Copy the URL by holding your finger in the address bar and then choosing Select All.

- Click on the download files icon to the right of the search window.

- Select new download.

- Paste the URL in the second window. To do this, hold your finger in the second window. When the magnifier is visible on the screen, move your finger and you will see the word Paste. Click on it.

- Name the file in the first window yourtitle.pdf. (Don't forget to add the .pdf extension.)

- Choose a location, if you have folders created.

Teachers and students can use Google to store PDF documents to share with the classroom. Other options upload audio/video created on a computer to Google and open and save it to a folder in Atomic Web Browser. This is a great collaboration tool. An "open documents" or "open audio" test could be created to be opened in one browser tab with a Google form for recording answers to be opened in another one. No Paper! This way of testing could be used in an art classroom with a picture opened in one tab for students to analyze historical and cultural aspects of artwork; the second tab could be a Google Form collecting data.

In geography, world history, or a social studies class, the answer sheet for a quiz goes in one tab and the questions, a map, a speech, or an image of an event goes in a second one (see Figures 6 and 7). A definition quiz could be easily created with definitions in one tab and the matching words in Google forms in a second one. The assessment items can be uploaded to Atomic Web Browser through iTunes.

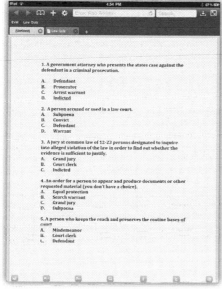

Figure 6—*Questions tab*

Figure 7—*Answer tab*

Box.net

App name: Box.net
Subject areas: Language arts, math, reading, social studies, and science
Available for: iPad / iPhone / iPod Touch
Cost: Free
Requirements: Requires iOS 3.0 or later.
iTunes URL: http://itunes.apple.com/us/app/box-net/id290853822?mt=8
Developer web site: http://www.box.net/
Internet required: Yes, but files can be downloaded for off-line viewing.

What Is Box.net?

Box.net is online storage (5GB) that allows you to view, access, and share files on your iPad, iPhone, and iPod Touch. This app can also be accessed from your normal computer and web browser by going to the www.box.net.

Box.net aids the way we work today, from collaborating with other teachers to providing digital content to students from anywhere, at any time. This tool lets you access your Box.net account directly through an iPad, iPhone, or iPod Touch. Teachers and students can have a shared workspace accessible from anywhere for documents, with 5GB of free cloud (online) storage for use with open documents, music, and videos.

Features

- Browse personal and shared files and folders (video documents, media, and many other files).

- Share files and folders with anyone with a direct link.

- Save files to access without Wi-Fi or data connection.

- Turn your folders into an online workspace where you can exchange feedback with teachers or students.

- Monitor updates to shared content.

- Open files in other apps on iPad.

- Set expiration dates for sharing and/or deleting documents from Box.net.

- Download Pages or Microsoft Word documents into Pages for iPad.

- Download Excel files into Numbers for iPad.

- Download Microsoft PowerPoint into Keynote for iPad.

- Open Box.net files in other programs such as iThoughts HD, Evernote, iBooks, and others (Figure 1).

- Print files from Box.net from Print n Share using a wireless printer.

Figure 1—Box.net program options

How Does Box.net Work?

Users will need to start by creating a Box account at www.Box.net. From the Box.net web site, files can be uploaded to Box for access from mobile devices. As shown in Figure 2, users can create folders to categorize documents and invite others to collaborate or view documents as well.

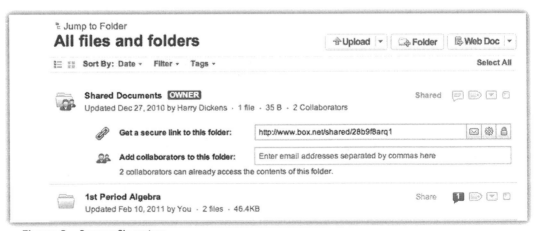

Figure 2—Box.net file options

By clicking on the word cloud at the top of the page, comments can be added in Box on the iPad, iPod Touch, or iPhone (as shown in Figure 3).

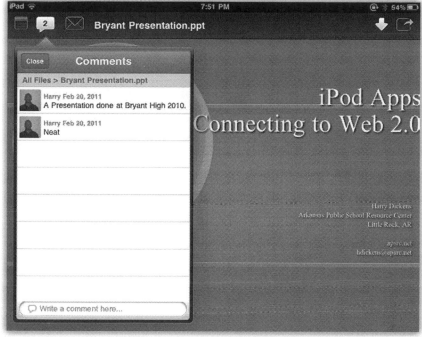

Figure 3—*Adding comments*

Files can be shared by clicking on the envelope at the top of the page; a link to the file is emailed to others (see Figure 4). Users can download or print when files are shared as a link. Documents can be shared via an Apple VGA adapter to a projector or television.

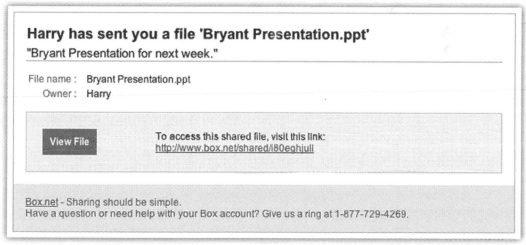

Figure 4—*Emailed file with link*

The app, when used on the iPad 2 / iPhone / iPod Touch 4th Generation, also allows users to upload photos from the camera roll or take a photo (Figure 5).

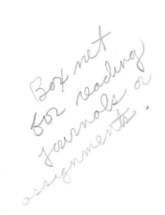

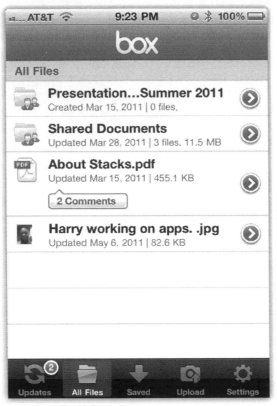

Figure 5—*Upload photos*

How Can Box.net Be Used in the Classroom?

Teachers have their own homework, with a seemingly endless stream of paperwork and communication. They must document many things and keep this information somewhere, often with limited network space to archive it. Box.net allows them to have a virtual file cabinet for archived documents. They also can use Box.net to share large digital images with students for a variety of visual classes or lessons, such as art history, painting, drawing, and sculpting. Box.net also allows the students and teachers to share files and documents. Using the online space the teacher can upload materials for the students to access and download. The students are able to select the file to download rather than the teacher pushing all of the files out to the students using a tool like email.

Box.net can be used as a tool for reflection. Users can draw understanding from a document or image that has been uploaded to Box.net and add comments about the document. Students can use the commenting feature to compare and contrast the experience of reading a story, drama, or poem with that of listening to or viewing an audio or video recording of the same piece. They could contrast what they "see" and "hear" when reading to when they listen or watch. This could be done with an individual, a small group, or even several small groups commenting on the same content. Students could compare and contrast a fictional portrayal of an event with a historical account of the same event as a means of understanding how fiction writers often use or alter history.

Teachers in science, history, literacy, and technical classes can use the commenting feature to allow students to provide a concluding statement or section that follows from and supports the information or explanation presented. Comments can be attached to any type of document. Figure 6 is a work of Huichol art, a jpeg image (http://farm1.static.flickr.com/22/27701692_c7daf4f50f.jpg): Students in an art class could comment on the use of color within the art and discuss the different artists who were creating this type of art.

Figure 6—*Huichol art comments*

In a history class, students can create comments on John F. Kennedy's inaugural address in response to a teacher's questions about the importance of inaugural addresses, the political messages behind them, and to whom the speech was really written (Figure 7).

Figure 7—*JFK inaugural speech comments*

Comments can be added on the iPad, iPod Touch, or iPhone or from a computer. In the classroom you could log into the same Box.net account and spread the collaboration or commenting on one topic to several devices.

GoodReader

App name: GoodReader for iPad
Subject areas: All
Available for: iPad
Cost: $4.99
Requirements: Compatible with iPad. Requires iOS 3.2 or later. For VGA out, an Apple iPad Dock Connector to VGA Adapter is required.
iTunes URL: http://itunes.apple.com/us/app/goodreader-for-ipad/id363448914?mt=8
Developer web site: http://www.goodreader.net/goodreader.html
Internet required: Yes, to connect to cloud servers

about the app

What Is GoodReader?

GoodReader is a file distribution and file management tool. The app is designed to read, show, and view almost any file you want to access from your iPad, iPod Touch, or iPhone.

GoodReader has the ability to display almost any file format as a PDF, including Microsoft Office documents, Pages, audio files, video files, and more. You can easily transfer files from PC or Mac computers. The first way to get files to your device is through the file-sharing feature in iTunes (see Figure 1).

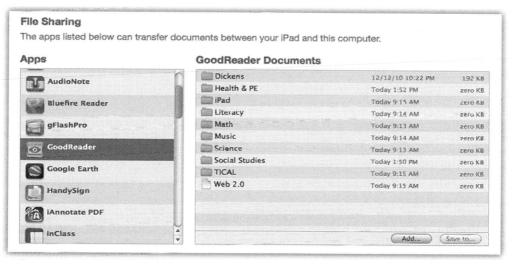

Figure 1—File sharing through iTunes

The second way is through a Wi-Fi transfer, shown in Figure 2. The third option, and the most advanced way, is by retrieving files from an online service such as Box.net, Dropbox, or Google Docs, as shown in Figure 3.

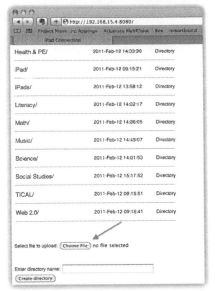

Figure 2—Wi-Fi transfer

Figure 3—Retrieving files online

A wonderful feature of this app is the ability to use it as a presentation tool with VGA out capability. With an Apple VGA adapter connected to a projector or television with VGA input, you can share files in GoodReader.

How Does GoodReader Work?

GoodReader works with or without the use of the Internet. You will need a sync cable to upload documents to the device with iTunes. To use the Wi-Fi feature for file sharing, you will need Internet access to connect to an online storage service.

How Can GoodReader Be Used in the Classroom?

In a classroom, GoodReader offers file management capabilities for the iPad, and presentation for most file types. The My Documents area of the app displays folders or files similar to what you see in My Documents on your computer (see Figure 4).

Once you tap on a folder and then tap on a document, you can display the document through a projector or just view it on the iPad's screen. Going green is possible with this app—tests, worksheets, or projects can be displayed via VGA directly from GoodReader. Documents with many pages can be scrolled through or searched by page number or keyword. Bookmarks can also be added to documents (see Figure 5).

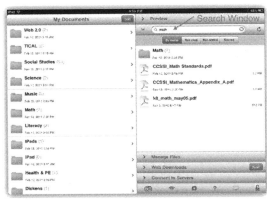

Figure 4—My Documents display

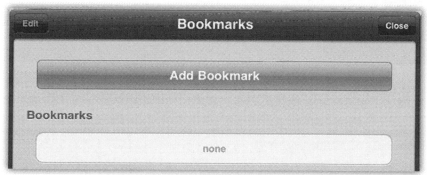

Figure 5—*Add bookmarks*

Storybooks, textbooks, or shared documents in PDF format are a great way to move to any section of the book. In landscape mode, two pages can be viewed at once (see Figure 6).

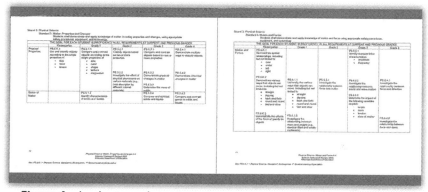

Figure 6—*Landscape mode two-page view*

Page orientation can be locked while viewing a document by clicking on the lock in the lower right corner of the screen. Saved web pages can be viewed full-screen (see Figure 7).

Figure 7—*Web page view*

GoodReader has a built-in web browser so web pages can be viewed or downloaded for viewing later. A sync feature syncs web pages to the most current view of the page. You can access documents through Wi-Fi transfer. However, this in not recommended for large documents.

From any computer, you can type in the address of the iPad to upload documents to. After typing in the address (typically similar to http://192.XXX.XX.X:8080), go to the bottom of the page and click on Choose Files. Your My Documents folder will open. Choose the file, and then click on Upload in the web browser (see Figure 8). The file is now in My Documents of the app. This means you can collect files from any computer that students may work on in class, and they simply upload the file in the same manner. This also means that, from the iPad, students can download documents that you want them to have access to.

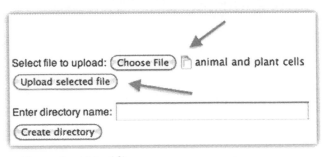

Figure 8—Upload files

With GoodReader, you also have access to photos and videos in your iPad's Photo Albums (see Figure 9). Another way of accessing documents you want to view on your iPad or display through your projector is through your online storage. Dropbox, Box.net, Google, and Mobile Me are the services you can use (see Figure 10).

Figure 9—Photo albums

Figure 10—Online storage options (1)

You can let the service store your password, or you can enter it each time you visit. Once you have connected, you can download from the online storage site (see Figure 11).

You can also upload from your device to the online storage site as well, which we cover in point form on the following page in the list for online storage. This will save storage space on the iPad.

Figure 11—Online storage options (2)

Transferring Files on the Device

Through iTunes

- Connect the device to your computer with your sync/charging cable.
- Go to iTunes, and then click on your device.
- Click on the apps icon on the top of the page, and then scroll to the bottom of the page.
- In the left window, you will find all of your apps that allow file transfer through iTunes.
- Click on GoodReader.
- In the window on the right, you can add documents.
- Click on Add and go to your My Documents to add the file you want on the iPad.
- Your file is now in the My Documents folder of GoodReader.

Through Wi-Fi

- Click on the Wi-Fi transfer icon.
- From any computer, type the IP address in your web browser.
- Click on Choose File.
- The My Documents folder on your computer will open.
- Choose the document.
- Your file is now in the My Documents folder of GoodReader.

Through Online Storage

- Click on Connect to Servers (see Figure 12).

Figure 12—Server connections

- Add the server.
- Name the server: enter your username (entering the password is optional).
- To access the server, click on the server login by entering your password (see Figure 13).
- Choose the file folder or file you want to download.
- Your file is now in the My Documents folder of your device.
- Uploading from the iPad to your online storage is also possible by clicking on the upload button, at the bottom of the window.

Figure 13—Password authorization

Preview Files

- Click on the files you want to open.
- Click on Preview; you will see a small image of the file (Figure 14).
- Tapping the document opens it.
- Clicking on Open In allows the document to be opened in other apps.

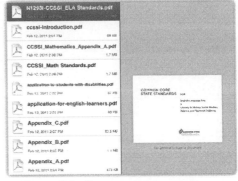

Figure 14—Document preview window

Find Files

- Click on Find Files (see Figure 15).
- Files can be searched by name, recently read, recently added, or starred.

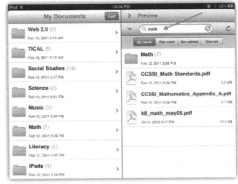

Figure 15—File search options

Manage Files

- Files can be starred (see Figure 16).
- Files can be password protected.
- Files can be marked read or unread.
- Files can be emailed.
- Files can be renamed.
- Folders can be created and loose documents can be moved to folders.
- Simple text files can be created; the Open In feature is here as well.
- Files can be deleted.

Figure 16—File managing options

Print n Share

App name: Print n Share
Subject areas: All
Available for: iPad / iPod Touch / iPhone
Cost: $8.99 for iPad / $6.99 for iPhone and iPod Touch
Requirements: Requires iOS 3.2 or later.
iTunes URL: http://itunes.apple.com/us/app/print-n-share-for-advanced/ id301656026?mt=8
Developer web site: http://mobile.eurosmartz.com/index.html
Internet required: Yes, for connection to cloud servers. Internet is also needed for Wi-Fi transfer.

What Is Print n Share?

Print n Share is an app that brings PC-printing functionality to the iPad. A wireless connection is needed for the app to print to wireless printers. WePrint printer server is needed to print to all printers.

How Does Print n Share Work?

To print using Print n Share directly, you'll need a wireless or Bluetooth-enabled printer. Indirectly, you can use any printer connected to a PC or Mac with the WePrint printer server installed, which is available as a free download right from the developer's web site (http://eurosmartz.com). Print n Share allows users on the same network to view and download documents on your device (Figure 1).

![Network sharing screenshot showing iPad interface with Network Sharing, Sharing: Documents, Connection addresses: http://Harry-Dickenss-iPad.local:8080 and http://192.168.15.14:8080, Stop Idle, Settings]

Figure 1—Network sharing

Access can be password protected. If users need to access documents on your local computer, this option is possible by connecting the iPad through WePrint on your computer (as shown in Figures 2 and 3).

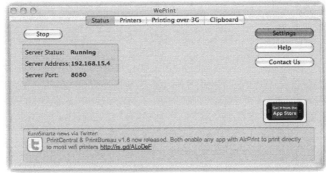

Figure 2—*WePrint connection*

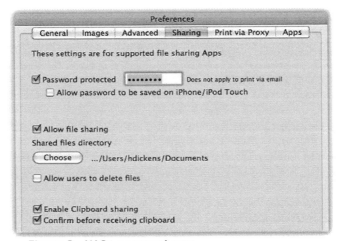

Figure 3—*WePrint password entry*

Folders can be shared (as shown in Figure 4).

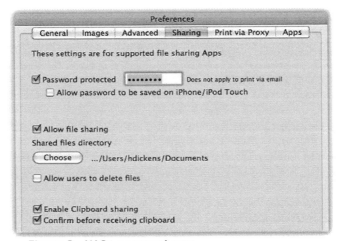

Figure 4—*File sharing*

Files in Box.net, iDisk files, and folders can be shared to Print n Share (Figure 5). It also has a built-in web browser (Figure 6), which allows users to print, bookmark, email, save as document, or save as image. The added functionality Print n Share brings to the iPad makes it a far more viable option as a laptop or netbook replacement.

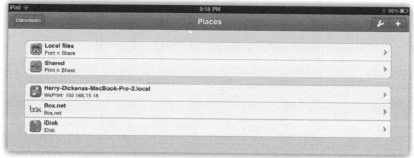

Figure 5—Sharing with Box.net and iDisk

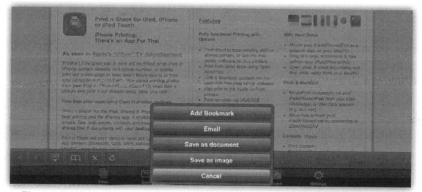

Figure 6—Web browser optons

How Can Print n Share Be Used in the Classroom?

Print n Share is the supreme printing app for the iPad, iPhone, or iPod Touch. Print n Share will enable you to print email, contacts, web pages, copied clips, email attachments, photos, text messages, shipping labels, and much more. Students and teachers can print pasted clips or store clips as files for archiving, previewing, emailing, and grouping. Files can be shared through a network for others to view them on other devices. Print n Share must run in the background on the iPad before printing from any of the programs mentioned above. Web browsers such as Atomic Web Browser and Safari print through Print n Share as well.

Other options for the classroom

- Transfer documents via iTunes
- Print from the photo gallery
- Save and print email attachments
- Transfer document to/from iPhone / iPod Touch
- Browse/transfer/print from Box.net (see Figure 5)

From the iPad 2, iPhone 3GS or 4, or the iPod Touch 4th generation, the app allows you to use the camera to take pictures for printing or emailing (Figure 7). This app could be used for gathering pictures during a scavenger hunt or from any of the other "places" in the app and saved later for printing.

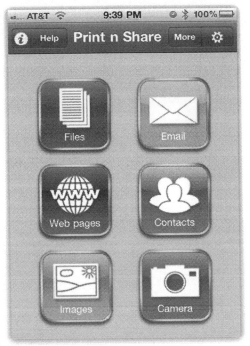

Figure 7—*Camera options*

After gathering information from a variety of sources, Print n Share can be used to print or email several documents at one time. If you are looking for a photo sharing tool for inside the classroom, Print N Share is an outstanding tool for collaborating, sharing, and connecting. In-app purchases can be made to link to a Dropbox or Google Docs account, FTP servers, and more. The in-app cost is $0.99.

Section 2

General APPS

Adobe Photoshop PS Express

App name: Adobe Photoshop PS Express
Subject areas: All
Available for: iPad / iPod Touch / iPhone
Cost: Free
Requirements: Requires iOS 4.2 or later.
iTunes URL: http://itunes.apple.com/ca/app/adobe-photoshop-express/
id331975235?mt=8
Developer web site: http://www.photoshop.com/products/mobile
Internet required: No

What Is Adobe Photoshop PS Express?

Adobe Photoshop PS Express is a limited feature set image editor available for the iPad, iPod Touch, and iPhone.

How Does Adobe Photoshop PS Express Work?

With an image that is imported (iPad 1) or taken using the built-in camera and stored in the photos container (iPhone, iPod Touch, and iPad 2), this application allows students to edit the image, adjust the features of the image, soften and sharpen focus, and apply effects and borders. The completed image can be saved locally on the device or uploaded to Adobe's Photoshop PS Express online space, Facebook, or tweet pictures.

Users load or take a picture and then select the editing tool they want to use. They make the adjustments to the image and finalize them by clicking OK. The Undo feature allows users to undo any changes that are not satisfactory. The basic editing tools (shown in Figures 1 and 2) include *crop, straighten, rotate,* and *flip.*

Figure 1*—Basic editing—crop*

The Adjust menu allows users to change the settings, balance the contrast, and adjust the exposure, saturation of colors, and so on. Sliding the finger left or right decreases or increases the percentage of change being applied. Here are your options:

- Contrast

- Saturation

- Tint

- Exposure

- Black and white

This feature set allows users to manipulate the image while experimenting with the different relative strengths of the adjustment at the stroke of a finger across the screen. Stroking the finger to the right-hand side increases the attribute and to the left decreases it. Once the adjustment is made, the OK button must be clicked to keep the changes.

Figure 2—*Basic editing—straighten*

The Effects menu has the border and effects options. This allows users to apply different border styles and add different filter effects (Figures 3 and 4).

Figure 3—*Effects options*

Figure 4—*Border options*

The effects available to users include Sketch, which applies a drawing-like filter to the image, as well as a selection of other filters and templates to manipulate the image. The border effect allows users to frame an image with a variety of different styles and appearances.

The saved image is stored in the pictures container in .jpg format, and can then be imported into a range of applications on the device including Pages, Keynote, Numbers, Comic Strip HD, and Comic Touch.

Advanced Uses

Adobe Photoshop PS Express has a number of classroom applications. As a simple and free editing tool for images, it can easily become a core component of the device. These basic, but straightforward, tools are unavailable in the photo library so users are unable to perform even the most basic of editing tasks, such as cropping, rotating, or flipping a photo. For the development of a word processing document, a presentation, or a comic/cartoon that requires images to be manipulated, this tool is ideal. The filters and effects allow users to customize the images to suit their needs and requirements, as by brightening a dull image or applying a colorful rainbow filter. As a result, Adobe Photoshop PS Express is usable and applicable to all subject areas that may use images and require these to be adjusted.

For students of photography and their teachers, this tool becomes more valuable. Students can quickly and easily adjust the contrast, exposure, saturation, and tint of photos to see the effect. The changes are easily replicable on full-versioned editors, allowing students in the field or the teacher demonstrating the effect to quickly and simply make changes.

Students learning about the levels of exposure can quickly create and save a series of images ranging from underexposed to overexposed, and then view these using the photo library. In a similar vein, they can adjust the saturation of color by moving their finger partly or completely across the screen. The proportion of the right-hand side of the screen the finger moves across gives the percentage increase and, inversely, the proportion of the left-hand side of the screen gives the percentage decrease in the saturation, exposure, and so on.

The in-app purchase of the Adobe Camera pack allows users to perform more advanced functions such as noise reduction, where even small flaws in the image are smoothed out, a self-timer tool for using the connected camera, and auto review, which allows you to preview and delete the image. These features are not yet supported on the iPad 2's camera.

Having a digital camera on the iPod Touch 4th Generation / iPhone is a benefit for any subject. Also, having an editing tool with a camera is even better. Students in the science classroom can use the Photoshop PS Express app to take pictures of data and edit them as soon as it is rendered to the iPod Touch / iPhone. Students in the social studies classroom can adjust content from their life or an environment with effects in the app, changing the tone of a picture before adding it to the camera roll (Figure 5). A story could be written with the tone of the image as part of the narrative.

Figure 5—Additional effects

After editing, the images are in the photo library of the iPad. These images can be imported into a Pages document or many other word processors on the iPad. In the English language arts classroom, students can take images, edit them, and use the photos to illustrate their words through a text document or one of the presentation tools on the device. The app can be used as a tool for comparing items side by side.

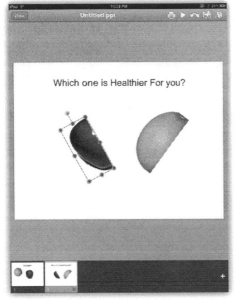 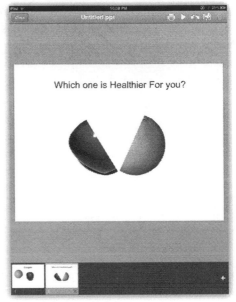

Figure 6—Imported photos with cropping *Figure 7—Final image*

Figures 6 and 7 show an apple and orange that have been cropped in Photoshop and imported into Quick Office. If you take a screen shot (by pressing and holding the home and pressing and releasing the power button), you will then need to use the Photoshop PS Express app to rotate any images you may want to place in other apps, such as StoryKit.

Dragon Dictation

App name: Dragon Dictation
Subject areas: All
Available for: iPad / iPod Touch / iPhone
Cost: Free
Requirements: Requires iOS 3.1 or later.
iTunes URL: http://itunes.apple.com/us/app/dragon-dictation/
id341446764?mt=8
Developer web site: http://www.dragonmobileapps.com/index.html
Internet required: Yes

What Is Dragon Dictation?

Dragon Dictation is a speech-to-text application. Students speak into the microphone and their speech is converted to text. Students can use Dragon Dictation to compose notes, write email messages, or send status updates to social networking accounts. Text also can be highlighted and pasted into another document.

How Does Dragon Dictation Work?

As notes are created, they appear in the window on the left (see Figure 1).

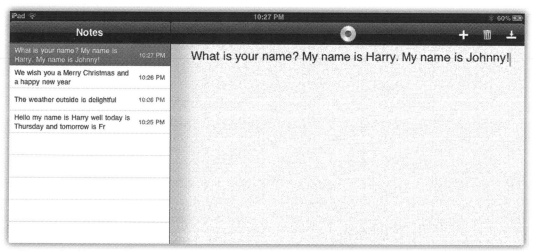

Figure 1—Notes window

To create a new note, click on the plus sign (+) on the right side of the window. To record, tap the record button in the top center. It will indicate that you are recording (Figure 2).

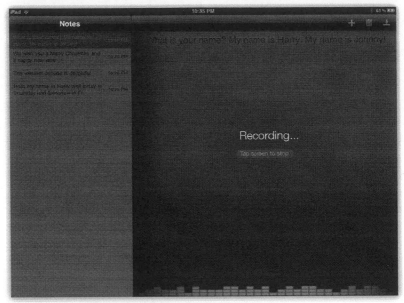

Figure 2—*Recording window*

When finished, tap the screen to end the recording. The text, which is processed on the Internet, can then be edited with the keyboard by tapping on the keyboard icon on the bottom center of the window, or text can be deleted by tapping on individual words (see Figure 3).

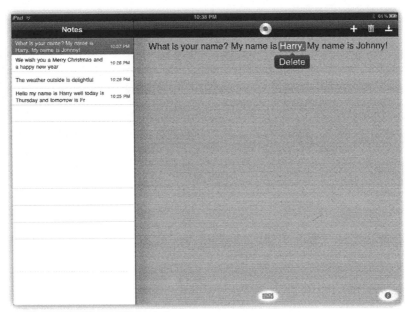

Figure 3—*Notes editing window*

Other options include sending the text to others via email, Facebook, or Twitter (shown in Figure 4). The cut and copy tools are also shown in Figure 4.

Figure 4—*Send to social networks*

The optional settings allow for auto signing in to Facebook and Twitter and include 11 other language options. Name recognition and the option to reset enrollment, which allows the app to reset your voice profile, are also available. Users can see other tips on using the app, including commonly used commands as well as commonly used punctuation, in Figure 5.

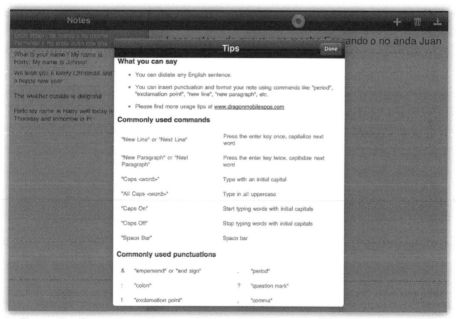

Figure 5—*Commonly used commands*

How Can Dragon Dictation Be Used in the Classroom?

Dragon Dictation is an easy-to-use voice recognition app that can be used for dictating messages for email and updates to Twitter and Facebook. Students who are reluctant to write or are having trouble getting thoughts out of their heads can use this app to speak their thoughts into an iPad, iPhone, or iPod Touch with an external mic. What is more amazing is that there is no need for any training. Nuance, the parent company of Dragon Dictation, uses cloud-based processing to capture the voice file, process it in the cloud, and return the transcription to the application in seconds.

Dragon Dictation is an outstanding accessibility tool and is great for those who are sight impaired and those who have difficulty with typing on a touch device or with communicating through text. Students can copy and paste their thoughts after speaking them into a document or presentation. The iPad app has a new feature that lets users easily view and manage texts for multiple documents. Notes are automatically saved so they can be edited or used at a later time. When students or teachers click on the Info button in the lower right corner of the app, tips for users open in another window.

Words for commonly used commands and commonly used punctuation marks are shared in the tips area. If students or teachers need a key to correct misspellings or add spaces or punctuation, a keyboard option at the bottom center of the iPad can be used after the recording has been stopped. Users can open Dragon Dictation on their device and begin to dictate. Within seconds the spoken words appear as text on the screen.

Advanced Uses

Users can copy and paste text into iTranslate to translate what they want to say into a different language or into StoryKit for storytelling. By changing the language setting, users can practice speaking in another language. Dragon Dictation can be used in the classroom to help students spell and write. Often, students who struggle with spelling have limited writing ability; this isn't because of a lack of deep thinking; it has more to do with the hesitancy to write what they can't spell. Students can easily practice spelling words using this app.

Dragon Dictation is a fantastic tool for brainstorming. Students can talk through an idea and have written notes with their thoughts to refer back to. They can also use the app to practice placing punctuation correctly in sentences.

Students need to be able to use technology strategically when creating, refining, and collaborating on writing. The Dragon Dictation application allows students to marshal their thoughts before speaking—especially students with writing problems or disabilities.

Students can use the Dragon Dictation app for taking "notes" for a research project in the library (Figures 6 and 7). Using Dragon Dictation, students could gather relevant information from multiple print and digital sources, use search terms effectively (with Dragon Search or other search engines), assess sources, and quote or paraphrase the data.

In a science class meeting outside, it may be easier for students doing research to speak the data they are collecting rather than trying to type it when working on a hands-on experiment.

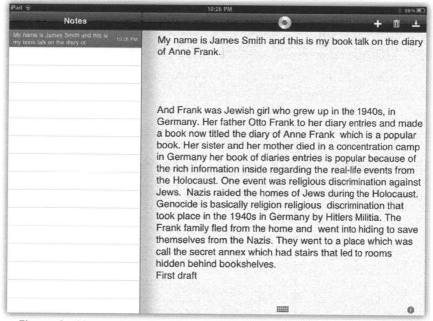

Figure 6—Notes with "Book talk"

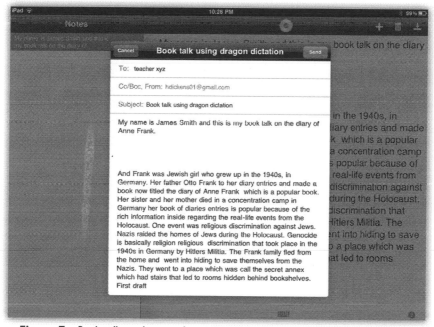

Figure 7—Book talk ready to send

eClicker Host/ eClicker

about the app

App name: eClicker Host/eClicker
Subject areas: All
Available for: iPad / iPod Touch / iPhone
Cost: $9.99
Requirements: Requires iOS 3.0 or later.
iTunes URL: http://itunes.apple.com/us/app/eclicker-host/id329199509?mt=8
Developer web site: http://www.eclicker.com/
Internet required: Wi-Fi is required.

What Is eClicker?

The eClicker app is a personal response system (PRS) that allows teachers to poll their class during a lesson. It provides them with the real-time feedback they need to be sure that students comprehend. The eClicker system is made up of two parts: the host and the client(s). Teachers use the host app to enter questions and begin the polling. Students participate in polls by entering the host's address in a web browser using any Internet-enabled device. Additionally, there is a free client app available for iOS devices that speeds up the process of connecting to a host through the Wi-Fi network.

How Does eClicker Work?

The eClicker app is a Wi-Fi-based app that allows up to 32 clients. This product consists of two parts: the host and the clients. The host, a purchased application, acts as a server that clients, which are free applications, connect to. On the host, the teacher develops and shares questions or polls. Students, as connected clients, answer the questions. The responses or answers are summarized by the host and can then be shared with the group.

On the host, the question editor works in either landscape or portrait mode (Figure 1). Teachers can edit questions on their iPads, iPhones, or iPod Touches or on their laptops or desktops using the eClicker editor web site (http://editor.eclicker.com).

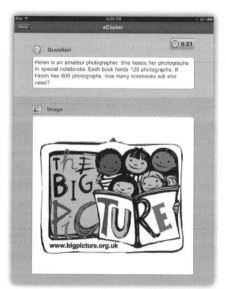

Figure 1—eClicker sample question

To create new questions, users click on the New Question icon in the upper right corner of the app (Figure 2).

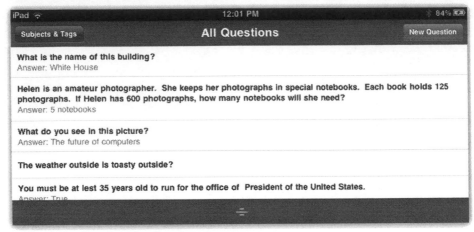

Figure 2—*Questions/New Question*

Each question can have up to five choices. The correct response can be labeled by tapping on the correct answer. True or false and agree or disagree can be answer choices. An answer explanation can be added as well, and the explanation displays after questions are answered. Questions can be tagged and a poll timer can be set from fifteen seconds to two minutes. The option to edit, duplicate, delete, and play the question are in the middle of the screen (Figure 3).

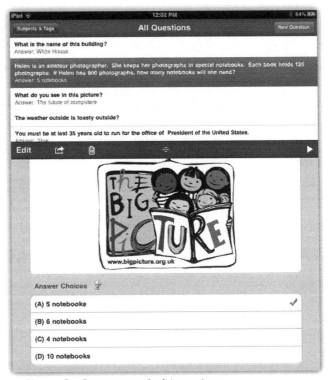

Figure 3—*Responses and editing options*

When client iOS devices open the eClicker client app, they can see the running host and can log in with their names (Figures 4 and 5). When play is clicked on the host device, a question is sent to the clients.

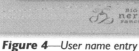

Figure 4—*User name entry*   **Figure 5**—*Sending a question*

How Can eClicker Be Used in the Classroom?

If you are a teacher or represent a school district looking for a PRS that will allow you to poll your students and receive real-time feedback, eClicker for your classroom or school is a good choice. This app offers a wide variety of educational uses in the classroom. Teachers can assess students' knowledge, engage students, access prior knowledge, quickly check for understanding, gather data through polls, preview and review content, and administer pop quizzes.

Once question sets are created, teachers can share them with other teachers via Bluetooth or any Wi-Fi-enabled device (please note that this feature is not supported on the first generation iPhone and iPod Touch). Questions can be given one at time by the teacher's control or as a set for more of an assessment-based option. An indicator can be displayed after each question that shows class rankings, which can either be turned on to create a more competitive game atmosphere or turned off to remove the competitive component. Teacher-created questions are stored separately from question sets so that they can be used in more than one question set; this allows teachers to easily modify lessons for different levels of classes.

Setting up a free account on the eClicker web site makes creating the questions very easy. To help differentiate instruction or add more information to a question, graphics can easily be added through an iPhone camera or an iPad / iPhone / iPod Touch photo library. An excellent feature of the most recent update of eClicker is the ability for teachers to annotate and draw images they can then use with their questions. The real-time feedback included in eClicker is an excellent way to find out which students are struggling in the class regardless of how proud or how reserved they may be. At the end of eClicker sessions, teachers can email a log of the eClicker session to themselves so that the data collected can be reviewed for out-of-class tutoring sessions.

Also, all of the historical polling data is saved for future viewing by the teacher. The eClicker app is a great way to use the iPhones and iPod Touches that are already in the pockets of your students and staff without the school district having to purchase the devices.

Another student response system that some may prefer is the iResponse Pro ($4.99). The iResponse Pro doesn't allow for images to be added to questions but it does allow for question to be sent to the iPad, iPod Touch, or iPhone as homework.

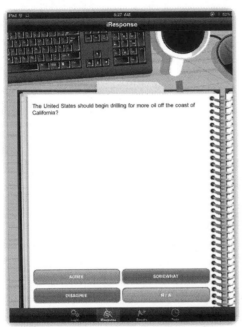

When the device connects to the teacher's computer the next day, the answers are collected. The take-home or out-of-class test can be timed too.

A great way to use the app is when the question that needs to be answered is outside the classroom—maybe in a library or a nature trail for a science classroom (Figure 6).

These clicker apps can be used during experiments, in research activities, for comparing products in an economics classroom, or as a planning and decision tool for any classroom. These are wonderful apps that allow you to leave the pencil-and-paper quizzes behind (Figure 7).

Figure 6—*iResponse—question for sending*

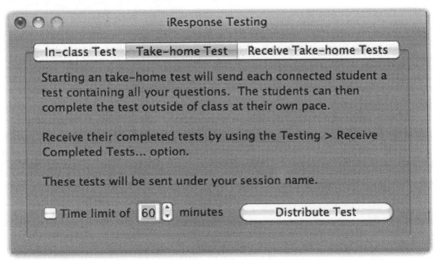

Figure 7—*iResponse testing feature*

Evernote

about the app

App name: Evernote
Subject areas: All
Available for: iPad / iPod Touch / iPhone
Cost: Free / Premium use $4.99/month or $44.99/year
Requirements: Requires iOS 3.0 or or later.
iTunes URL: http://itunes.apple.com/us/app/evernote/id281796108?mt=8
Developer web site: http://www.evernote.com/
Internet required: Only for synchronization

What Is Evernote?

Evernote allows a user to create an online notebook from text, handwritten notes, audio clips, web pages, and more.

How Does Evernote Work?

The Evernote app runs directly from the iPod Touch, iPhone, iPad, and computer. Internet connectivity is not required for the app to work but is required for synchronization. To take notes, users click on the new note icon at the bottom left of the screen (Figure 1).

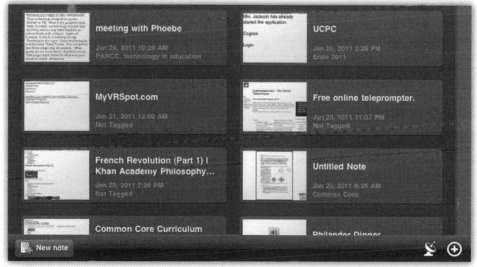

Figure 1—*New note option*

Users then title the note, assign it to a notebook, and add tags. Notebooks and tags also have a dropdown window, which allows users to quickly make notebook and tag choices. On the iPad, audio notes can be recorded while users are taking notes, and with iPad 2, snapshots can be taken with the camera. Users tap on the microphone icon at the top of the screen for this option. Images can be added by tapping on the pictures icon at the top of the screen as well. After finishing a note, simply click Save.

Figure 2 shows a note in edit view with audio and image clips. Audio and images clips can be removed by tapping or holding your finger on the clip. Editing text works the same way—just tap and hold and the keyboard appears. Figure 3 shows a note in view mode with images, text, and audio.

Figure 2—New note in edit view

Figure 3—New note in view mode

At the bottom of the screen, there are some noted options—new, refresh, delete, email, print, sync, and additional features in the Evernote "trunk" edit. Users can view notes in several different views. In Figure 4, the notes are in notebooks view. Notes can be tagged (Figure 5) and viewed by locations when location services are turned on.

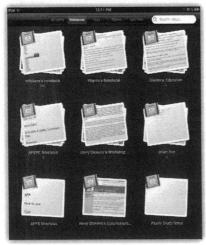

Figure 4—Evernote notebooks

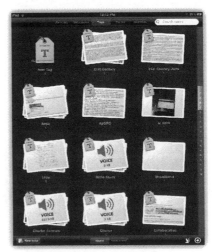

Figure 5—Evernote note tags

In the places view, users can tap and scroll around the map notes for map locations that are visible at the top of the screen. Searches can be saved to quickly find notes for later viewing or editing.

How Can Evernote Be Used in the Classroom?

Evernote is one of the most useful productivity apps because it can be used on mobile devices as well as via the web from any computer. With Evernote, students with an iPhone or iPod can upload text, snapshots, or voice memos into the app. Ninety-minute chunks of audio lecture notes can now be recorded into Evernote. Students can create to-do lists, jot down random thoughts, leave a voice memo, and more. With a free Evernote account, users can access all versions of Evernote on an iPad, iPhone, iPod Touch, or computer. Notes can be synchronized, but are limited to images, audio links, and PDF. Notes can be shared for read-only access.

Students can use Evernote to keep track of their notes, research, homework, tests, quizzes, and anything else that is school related. Revision history can be tracked on all notes. Evernote on the iPod Touch, iPhone, and iPad 2 allows users to capture pictures of almost anything they wish to remember, such as a snapshot from a teacher's whiteboard or picture text and audio during a scientific experiment. In a few quick, short steps, those pictures can be saved into Evernote, organized, and given a brief description, making the picture easily accessible in the future. Evernote has made the organizational hassle of being a student much easier.

Evernote is on the Internet, and students can easily access their Evernote information from anywhere on any computer with an Internet connection. Pencast from Livescribe pens can now be loaded into Evernote. Livescribe pens are used to create handwritten notes with audio on special paper. Video or snapshots can be taken through the iSight camera with the application when downloaded and used on an Apple computer. With Evernote, students can create notebooks inside the app; for example, they can have six notebooks for a six-period day. Inside each notebook, students can tag notes. For example, inside an Algebra notebook, students can have tags for homework, classwork, glossary terms, video notes, and so on. With a premium account, which costs $5 per month, students can share and edit notes with someone, making Evernote an excellent collaboration tool. Students can also upload text or pictures to an Evernote account through an Evernote email account (such as user@m.evernote.com).

GarageBand

App name: GarageBand
Subject areas: Performing arts, language arts, and so on
Available for: iPad / iPod Touch / iPhone
Cost: $4.99
Requirements: Requires iOS 4.2 or later.
iTunes URL: http://www.apple.com/ipad/from-the-app-store/garageband.html
Developer web site: http://www.apple.com/
Internet required: No

about the app

What Is GarageBand?

GarageBand is a purchased app developed by Apple. It is a music creation tool with a voice recording facility, which is useful for creating soundtracks and recording podcasts.

How Does GarageBand Work?

GarageBand for the iPad is the equivalent of GarageBand for the standard Apple laptop or desktop. This versatile tool allows users to create and compose music using a wide range of instruments. The application also includes a sampler and audio recorder (Figure 1). The sampler allows users to create an instrument from a series of sounds they record. This instrument is then played using a keyboard.

Figure 1—*GarageBand home screen*

GarageBand allows users to select from a range of tools and instruments to develop and publish musical compositions and podcasts. The ability to layer multiple recordings or tracks (GarageBand supports up to eight tracks) allows the creative user to develop products of high complexity and detail. The loops-based tool enables users to create music by accessing the library of more than 200 loops and arranging these into a suitable composition.

The application supports multitouch, allowing depth and accuracy when playing or strumming instruments. The recording facility allows users to have up to eight tracks being played at once. Each track is developed independently, and students then construct their final product by layering the different voices, whether they are instrumental or vocal, and professionally developing loops. The drum machine shown in Figure 2 is an example of how music can be easily composed using GarageBand.

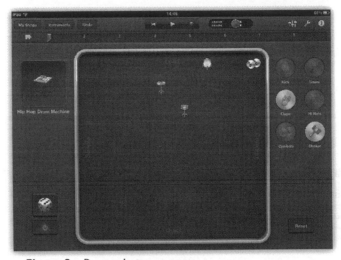

Figure 2—*Drum selector screen*

Vocals can be recorded using the built-in microphone. Completed files can be exported via email or iTunes, and products being developed can be transferred between GarageBand on the iPad and Apple computers.

Figure 3—*Audio recorder screen*

The audio recorder (Figure 3) allows users to develop podcasts and record their own instruments. Users can record with the built-in microphone, the audio port, or specialized adapters.

How Can GarageBand Be Used in the Classroom?

With a connection to the Internet and a computer, students can quickly and easily surf and download music. More often than not, the music they obtain is pirated or stolen. GarageBand presents an easy and engaging alternative to music piracy. In the media studies classroom, students are asked to design and develop a short advertisement that will appeal to their target audience of high school age students. Since the students must create all of the elements of the product, they cannot download music files from the Internet to embed in their video. The students construct the backing track using the wide variety of loops in GarageBand. They select the style and genre of the music and are able to quickly construct a percussion track and add a bass and lead guitar accompanied by a synthesizer. The end product is a unique music track constructed for a specific purpose by students with little or no musical training.

GarageBand also lends itself to developing and editing podcasts. Using the built-in microphone or connecting a microphone to the iPad via the audio port, students are able to record, edit, and manipulate audio recordings. Using short 10- to 15-second sound bites, students can work through their script, discarding the bites of poorer quality and keeping the recordings that are free of "ummms" and "ahhhs." Once the base track is assembled, they add in audio effects, such as short piano snippets, to indicate the end of the section and percussion elements to emphasise the key statements. The more able students use the loops to develop a backing track to play as background music.

In the music class, GarageBand allows students to compose and play their compositions using a variety of instrumental voices. The musically adept students are able to use multitouch to play multiple keys on the keyboard or chords using smart chords on stringed instruments. The simple touch-based input allows quick and easy composition and experimentation.

Garageband has a wide range of instruments and voices that can be selected and used for music composition, as shown in Figure 4.

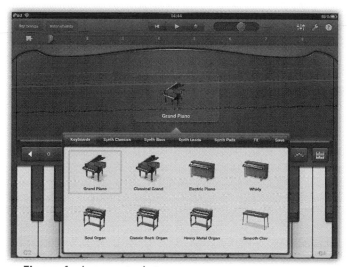

Figure 4—*Instrument selector*

Google Earth

App name: Google Earth
Subject areas: Social sciences, geography
Available for: iPad / iPod Touch / iPhone
Cost: Free
Requirements: Requires iOS 3.0 or later.
iTunes URL: http://itunes.apple.com/us/app/google-earth/id293622097?mt=8
Developer web site: http://www.google.com/mobile/iphone/
Internet required: Yes

What Is Google Earth?

Google Earth is a geographical information system (GIS). The software installed on the device acts as a client connecting to the Google servers and presents the requested location. The location can be viewed as satellite images and aerial photographs with maps overlaid on the location.

How Does Google Earth Work?

Google Earth allows users to navigate in a variety of methods. They can enter a location in the search field, they can move to the location using gestures to navigate and zoom in or out, or if auto-tilt is enabled, they can tilt the iPad to give direction and zoom. Sliding two fingers up and down the image will change the angle of view, and double tapping on the location will zoom in. A two-fingered double tap will zoom out. The layers tool enables the basic GIS feature. By selecting and deselecting the layers, you can toggle on or off overlays such as

- Places
- Businesses
- Panoramic photos (uploaded by other users and geotagged to the location)
- Wikipedia links
- Borders and labels
- Roads
- Oceans

How Can Google Earth Be Used in the Classroom?

Google Earth allows quick and efficient access to a range of information. Using the layers you can quickly and easily fly to faraway places or simply find where you currently are (this requires the position tool in Options to be switched on).

In the classroom, the easy navigation using the gestures makes accessing information simple for students of all ages. Using tilt (sliding two fingers up and down the image to tilt the viewing angle) and terrain enable students to quickly grasp the contours and layout of the location (shown in Figure 1).

In social studies and humanities, Google Earth brings maps to life. Students are able to quickly move to the location being studied and gain an instant perspective using the search feature or by navigating using gestures. The geo-located images, linked to the pages, appear as hotspots students are able to open and browse. The link to Wikipedia articles that relate to the image provide an information source about the site and links to further resources. The Wikipedia articles and images open within the application, minimizing downtime swapping between the GIS viewer and the information resource.

Figure 1—*Google Earth view options*

Figure 2—*Layers screen*

The layers available within Google Earth are simple but do provide a useful tool set (see Figure 2). Layers in Google Earth are toggled on or off by clicking the Layers button and selecting and deselecting the layers wanted. In the languages classroom, Google Earth provides an insight into other countries. A large element of learning a language is learning about the culture. While it would be ideal for students to visit and immerse themselves in the culture of another country, this is not always practical.

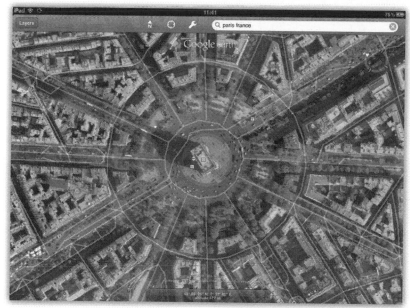

Figure 3—*Roads layer/Arc de Triomphe aerial image*

Figure 3 illustrates an aerial view of the Arc de Triomphe with the roads layer enabled. Using the aerial imagery and layers in Google Earth, students are able to visualize the scenes and location they are studying. For example, students studying France would be able to view the Arc de Triomphe, the Avenue des Champs Élysées, and the Eiffel Tower from a variety of angles and perspectives, making for a far more memorable and powerful classroom experience than a discussion alone.

iBooks

about the app

App name: iBooks
Subject areas: All
Available for: iPad / iPod Touch / iPhone
Cost: Free
Requirements: Requires iOS 4.0 or later.
iTunes URL: http://itunes.apple.com/us/app/ibooks/id364709193?mt=8
Developer web site: http://support.apple.com/kb/HT4059
Internet required: Yes, to purchase and download content

What Is iBooks?

iBooks enables users to download gorgeous, full-page illustrated children's books, cookbooks, and art books, or flip through Enhanced Books, where words, pictures, audio, and video come together. Listen to an author read a favorite passage, watch supplementary video, or view a library of photos or unpublished excerpts (http://www.apple.com/ipad/built-in-apps/ibooks.html).

How Does iBooks Work?

Books from the iBookstore can only be downloaded with an Apple ID in either eBook or PDF format. Figure 1 shows the bookshelf view of a book collection.

Figure 1—iBooks bookshelf

There is a search window to search all of your collections to find a book, PDF, or ePub document. With a tap, it flips around to reveal the iBookstore (see Figure 2), where you'll find more than 200,000 books—many of them free. View what's featured on the iBookstore and the *New York Times* bestseller lists or browse by title, author, or genre. When you find a book you like, tap to see more details, peruse reviews, or even read a free sample. Once a book is downloaded, it appears on your bookshelf. Users can email their notes created while reading a book or email and print from PDF documents.

Figure 2—*iBooks bookstore*

How Can iBooks Be Used in the Classroom?

Apple's iBooks is a base application that enables users to discover, browse, and download ebooks right to their iPad, iPhone, or iPod Touch. Users can browse the table of contents of a book, adjust the brightness, and change the font size and style. Sepia can be turned on or off. Users can search with the spotlight feature while reading a book. Google and Wikipedia searches are also possible within the app. Bookmarks, as well as where a reader stopped reading, are set automatically as long as there is Internet service available for the device.

When a word is highlighted in an ebook, users can either copy for another application, look up the word in the dictionary, highlight it along with a note, or search for the word in other sections of the book. Books can be added from the iBookstore or through the App Store in iTunes. Unlike traditional textbooks, notes can be added to any book, PDF, or ePub document (see Figure 3).

Figure 3—*Adding a note*

With iBooks there are limitless opportunities for students and teachers to import PDF documents into iBooks or drag and drop PDF documents into the library area of iTunes. Creating electronic books is possible with Apple's word processor Pages. Students and teachers can create eBooks with audio, video, and weblinks.

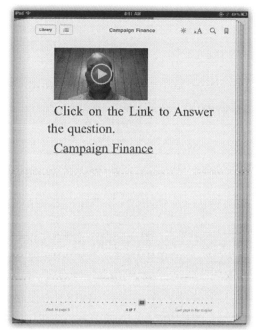

Figure 4—*Example of video web link*

Figure 4 shows an example of a user-created ePub document about campaign finance. In this clip there is a video created from the computer as well a web link to a Google form to answer a question. The creator of the eBook would simply drag and drop the eBook into the library of iTunes. Using this feature, students could create a documentary and have audio and video resources inside their book. Using iBooks in this fashion is a great way to build collaborative projects as well as give students an opportunity to share what they know about a topic in a digital way.

Teachers can create or convert the handouts that are required for their classroom to eBooks for students. Using the options from Pages for adding images, video, and web links to other sources or even quizzes, the teacher is teaching the way the digital natives want to be taught and allowing students to use the tools they use every day. With some guidance and support from peers and adults, students can use iBooks as a place to store their writings. They can also use iBooks with the Internet to produce and publish their own writing and present the relationships between information and ideas efficiently as well as to interact and collaborate with others. New technologies like iBooks and the ePub format have broadened and expanded the role that speaking and listening play in acquiring and sharing knowledge and have tightened their link to other forms of communication. The Internet has accelerated the speed at which connections between speaking, listening, reading, and writing can be made, requiring that students be ready to use these modalities nearly simultaneously. Imagine students not just using a word processor to create the writing, but to create a document with video and web links that you can visit with a click.

Technology itself is changing quickly, creating a new urgency for students to be adaptable in response to change. Integrating multimedia and visual displays into presentations to clarify information, strengthen claims and evidence, and add interest can only make the reading and writing more enjoyable. And using the accessibility tools of the iPad, iPod Touch, or iPhone, the words on the pages can come to life. To get to the accessibility tools, go to the general settings of the device (Figure 5) and click on accessibility on the lower right side of the page.

Using the web site Lit2Go (http://etc.usf.edu/lit2go/), users can find a range of text types, with texts selected from a broad range of cultures and periods. These PDF documents can then be downloaded into iBooks.

Figure 5—*General settings*

Please remember to do the following if you plan to use the site:

- *Educational Use*—A maximum of twenty-five (25) MP3 and/or text files may be used in any noncommercial, educational project (report, presentation, display, web site, etc.) without special permission. The use of more than 25 MP3 and/or text files in a single project requires written permission from the Florida Center for Instructional Technology (FCIT) at USF.

- *Credit*—Please credit FCIT whenever a resource is used. If resources from this site are incorporated into a web site, a link to http://etc.usf.edu/lit2go must be included on your site.

(Please note that because of copyright agreements and restrictions, iBooks may only be purchased in some countries.)

iMovie

about the app

App name: iMovie
Subject areas: All
Available for: iPad 2 / iPod Touch 4th Generation / iPhone 4
Cost: $4.99
Requirements: Requires iOS 4.2.6 or later.
iTunes URL: http://itunes.apple.com/us/app/imovie/id377298193?mt=8
Developer web site: http://www.apple.com/support/iphone/imovie/
Internet required: Yes, for sharing movies

What Is iMovie?

iMovie is a video editing software app that allows Mac, iPod Touch 4th generation, iPhone 4, and iPad 2 users to edit their own videos.

How Does iMovie Work?

The first screen in iMovie has six icons from which to choose at the bottom of the screen (Figure 1).

Figure 1—iMovie home screen

The first icon is the help menu (Figure 2). Clicking on the plus sign (+) starts the process of creating a new movie from files on the computer or the camera on the device being used.

Figure 2—Help screen

The icons on this screen include a button that takes you back to the front page and an audio button for voice-over. The last button on the left allows users to import movies, still shots, and audio from the photo library (Figure 3).

Figure 3—Import options

Project settings are on the right side of the screen, including the project theme, looping music, and fading options (Figure 4). The video icon for recording and the play button are the last two buttons on the right side of the screen. After importing images or video, pinching and zooming can be done by tapping on the photo or video clip (Figure 5).

Figure 4—Project settings

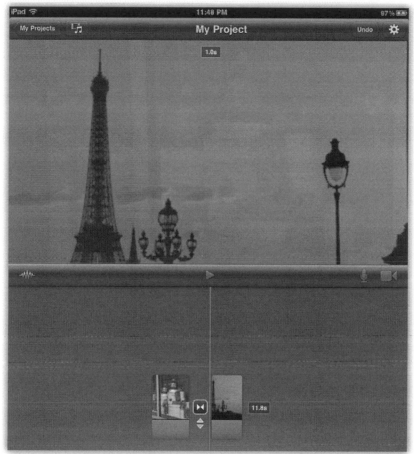

Figure 5—*Video clip import*

Double tapping allows users to add a title as well as a location. Users can double click on the transition icon to change transition style and time between transitions (Figure 6).

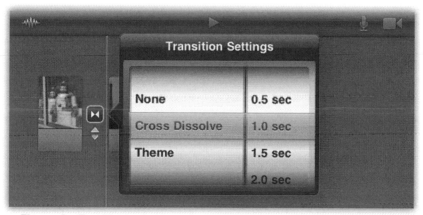

Figure 6—*Transition settings*

How Can iMovie Be Used in the Classroom?

Like all educational technology, desktop video editing is not a ubiquitous solution for all of the challenges teachers face in today's classroom. Using digital video encourages individual expression and creativity, revitalizes content, promotes collective knowledge construction and individual reflection, and offers students of a variety of backgrounds and experiences the opportunity to engage in authentic learning.

With iMovie, teachers can bring lessons to life through video, sound, and pictures. iMovie is a powerful and highly engaging tool for students to share their knowledge and express themselves in the form of digital movies. Students can create high-quality video reports to demonstrate abstract concepts or documentaries to increase the relevance of social issues. And teachers can easily share best classroom practices with peers. Students can create compelling projects that combine digital video, photos, music, and even their own voice narration. There's no limit to what they can create. In English language arts, students can use research skills to locate information on the Internet about a book and author they are highlighting. Then students use this information to write scripts that they will read as other students use their technology skills to videotape them. Students learn to use a digital video and still camera as they work on the project. Research skills, writing and reading skills, real-world use of technology, and video editing skills are used by students in order to complete their iMovie. Here are some other ideas for using iMovie in the classroom:

- To capture and assess oral readings
- To expose students to different types of culture by creating video documentaries
- To create a movie that depicts different parts of speech
- To produce a videocast about current events
- To create a digital book summary
- To create a movie on life skills

New technologies have broadened and expanded the roles that speaking and listening play in acquiring and sharing knowledge and have tightened their link to other forms of communication. Digital content confronts students with the potential for continually updated content and dynamically changing combinations of words, graphics, images, hyperlinks, and embedded video and audio.

Using an app like iMovie, students can make strategic use of digital media and visual displays of data to express information and enhance peer as well as their own understanding of a presentation. Students can gather relevant information from multiple print and digital sources; for example, trials for a science project can be made into videos and merged together with other digital text as a part of the project.

Teachers and students can turn existing Keynote presentations into movies that can be merged with new content. In the social studies classroom, students can create and document accounts from the past and include videos, digital still shots, and audio from speeches or writing from the founding fathers and other historical figures in their presentations. Since music is such an important part of students' lives, it should be allowed when appropriate to the content.

In a class that may required investigative research, iMovie can be the aggregator that puts all the pieces of the research together. Movies can be uploaded to YouTube or Vimeo for online viewing and be critiqued by people from outside the brick-and-mortar school. Using iMovie, the possibilities are endless for many subject areas.

iThoughtsHD

App name: iThoughtsHD
Subject areas: All
Available for: iPad
Cost: $9.99
Requirements: Requires iOS 4.2 or later.
iTunes URL: http://itunes.apple.com/us/app/ithoughtshd-mindmapping/
id369020033?mt=8
Developer web site: http://www.ithoughts.co.uk
Internet required: Not for use, but yes for sharing maps

What Is iThoughtsHD?

The iThoughtsHD app is a mind-mapping, brainstorming, graphical organizing tool available for the iPad. Mind maps and brainstorms of considerable complexity can be easily created and manipulated using iThoughtsHD. Here's an example in Figure 1.

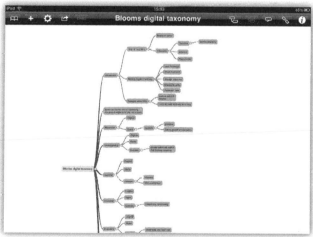

Figure 1—*Zoomed-out mind map*

This tool allows students to enter a central topic and then add sibling and daughter nodes as required. The nodes can be edited and customized using color, icons, and shape of the node. You can add notes to each node. Once the map is developed, the position of the nodes and their subordinates can be easily adjusted and manipulated. Links can be made between different nodes and can be customized to show different color and line ending and starting styles. Users can select backgrounds for their mind map and different font sizes, and they can also relate color to nodes and assign icons.

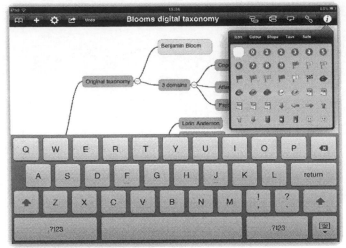

Figure 2—*Editing nodes*

There are more than 90 icons that can be added to the map to add structure and function, including the six thinking hats icons (see Figure 2). This app also has a limited project management capability with tasks being assigned to nodes, along with the ability to set level of completion for each task. Mind maps can be exported in a wide range of formats, including

- PDF—Adobe portable document format

- .mm format—free mind

- .opml—OPML format

- .nm—nova mind format

- .mmap—mind manager format

- .imm—imindmap format

- .Cdmz—concept draw format

The completed maps can be emailed from the program or uploaded to iDisk, transferred by Wi-Fi, or uploaded to a number of web sites (see Figure 3).

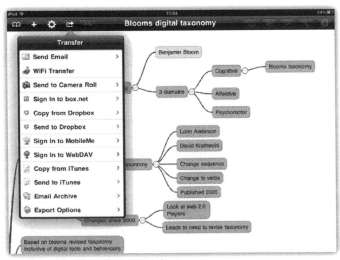

Figure 3—*Transferring and sharing*

How Can iThoughtsHD Be Used in the Classroom?

Mind-mapping tools can be used in all subject areas. The mind map allows students to link between concepts and display relationships. For visual learners, mind maps are a preferred tool as students are able to quickly and easily see the primary relationships and then the links between concepts and ideas.

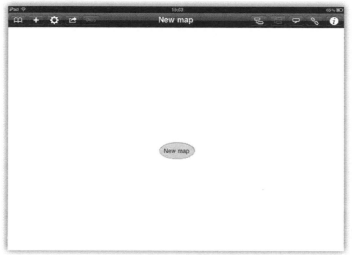

Figure 4—*Adding a new map*

New maps are quickly and easily created and older maps can be accessed using the app (Figure 4). The iThoughtsHD app is a powerful tool for note taking. Users can quickly add daughter nodes and sibling nodes by clicking on the buttons on the toolbar (see Figure 5). They can link nodes to show relationships and link concepts. It makes a powerful tool for taking notes in meetings and developing project plans from them. By identifying different items and then stating level of completion, users can measure the progress of individual components of the project as well as the project as a whole.

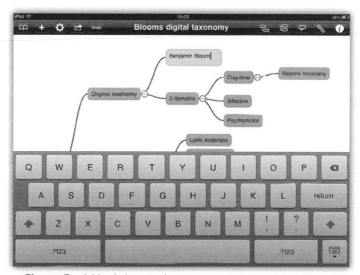

Figure 5—*Adding/editing nodes*

When brainstorming, users are able to quickly enter multiple ideas and then sort and organize them. They can then draw links between the ideas. Using the icons, users can set priority or ranking as well as flag specific nodes. Users are also able to add details to nodes. Editing nodes is straightforward. Clicking on a node allows users to edit the node, and using the new sibling or child buttons allows users to create further nodes on the same or a subordinate level.

Brainstorming tools can be used for analysis and evaluation. DeBono's thinking hats icons allow students to use the six thinking hats to analyze the issue, problem, or concept from the different perspectives of this widely used tool.

- *Black hat*—Negative aspects

- *White hat*—Information and facts

- *Red hat*—Emotions

- *Blue hat*—Thinking, metacognition

- *Green hat*—Creativity

- *Yellow hat*—Positive aspects

Similarly, users can use the reflective cycle to apply higher-order thinking to problems. These are the stages of the reflective cycle:

- *Define*—Asking the descriptive questions relating to the topic: what, where, when, and who.

- *Analyze*—Asking the deeper questions of why and how.

- *Evaluate*—Drawing from the definition and analysis, learners examine the impact, importance, effectiveness, and relationships within and around the concept.

- *Transform*—Deciding waht to do from here.

iTranslate/ iTranslate Plus

App name: iTranslate & iTranslate Plus
Subject areas: All
Available for: iPad / iPod Touch (iTranslate for iPad) / iPhone (iTranslate Plus)
Cost: Free with advertisements for basic version / $1.99 for iTranslate Plus
Requirements: iTranslate for iPad: iOS 3.2; iTranslate Plus: iOS 3.0
iTunes URL: http://itunes.apple.com/us/app/itranslate-free-translator/ id288113403?mt=8
Developer web site: http://sonicomobile.com/itranslate-ipad/
Internet required: Yes

What Is iTranslate?

iTranslate (for iPad and iPod Touch) and iTranslate Plus (for iPhone) are powerful translation tools. Users enter text in a variety of languages (approximately 50 at the time of this writing) and this app will instantly translate the text into a second language. It also has a sound playback.

How Does iTranslate Work?

The language recognition feature in the iPad allows unknown text to be entered and translated into the language of choice. Users are able to listen to sound playback in both the language in which the phrase or word was entered and the translated language.

In iTranslate Plus (iPhone and iPod Touch), the voices need to be purchased and downloaded. There are different regional versions within a language; for example, in French there are French voices and Canadian French voices. This app for iPad offers 11 different free text-to-speech voices: English, French, German, Chinese (traditional and simplified), Italian, Japanese, Korean, Russian, Spanish, and Portuguese (Figure 1).

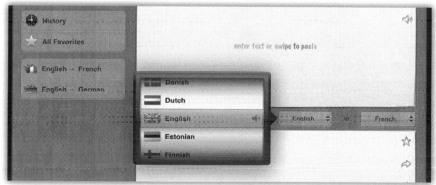

Figure 1—*Language choices*

The vocabulary and its translation can be compiled into lists for later use. Users can add a favorite word, phrase, or body of text to a specific list; for example, English–German or English–French (Figure 2).

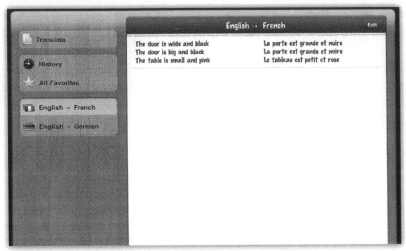

Figure 2—*Lists in iTranslate*

These lists can be recalled and edited at will. Using the edit function, lists can be selected, modified, and emailed to recipients as required. From the translation panes and the lists, translated phrases can be emailed as well (Figure 3).

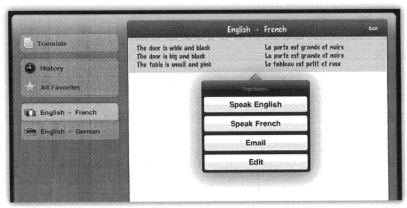

Figure 3—*Editing lists*

How Can iTranslate Be Used in the Classroom?

The iTranslate app has a variety of applications in the classroom. The first use is translation of words and phrases using the wide selection of languages available. Large sections of text can be selected and pasted into the entry pane and quickly translated into the selected language (see Figures 4 and 5). Entered text can be added to a list of translated words or phrases and saved for future reference and use. This feature allows users to compile their own dictionary of words and phrases that they can refer to. In supported languages they can also listen to the spoken version of the saved vocabulary.

Figure 4—*Text entry*

Multiple translation lists can be used, enabling different language classes to develop their own lists. The ability to email lists allows students to share their lists and translations, as well as send material to their teacher.

Figure 5—*Entered text for multiple lists*

The tool can also be used as a language validation tool. Selecting or entering a passage in the language being learned and then translating it to the native tongue of the user will show simple mistakes and grammatical errors within the limitations of the application. The application provides immediate feedback as the text is translated instantly as it is entered.

The spoken component allows users to enter text and translate it into the language of choice and then listen to the spoken version in both the language of entry and translation. This allows users to associate both the written form of the language and the spoken version. With iTranslate Plus, the user can purchase regional languages such as Canadian French and standard French.

The portability of the iPad, iPod Touch, and iPhone allows iTranslate to be used while you are traveling. Entering the text on signs, menus, and notices and then translating it into your native tongue provides a simple and portable solution to understanding written text.

Similarly, entering the phrase you wish to say to a person and listening to the translated spoken phrase facilitates communication and provides success in speaking the language. The regional variations of languages also assist in accurate communication.

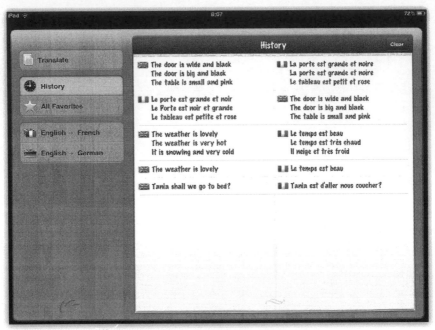

Figure 6—*History feature screen*

Students in an English language arts class could translate poems and other writings written in a different language into their own.

Another classroom application would be to have multilingual classes translate texts into their native language, then give literal translations back into English. The iTranslate app would assist with this project. Students could use the app to assist them in fixing a bad translation into English. Since music is such an integral part of today's students' lives, have them translate songs into different languages. Have the students write subtitles for a television clip using iTranslate to translate words they may not have studied yet or if they are not sure which word to use as part of the subtitle.

Students could use iTranslate to assist with the translating of newspaper stories for the school. This could also be used as a conversation trigger for newspaper articles written in one language and discussed in another one. iTranslate could be useful in those situations in which students may not know the word(s) they want to use. In a social studies classroom, instead of students simply reading about another culture, iTranslate would allow them to converse via email with someone who lives in that culture but may not speak their language.

Keynote

about the app

App name: Keynote
Subject areas: All
Available for: iPad / iPod Touch / iPhone
Cost: $9.99
Requirements: Connection to a projector or monitor requires a VGA
break-out cable; iOS 4.2.8 or later.
iTunes URL: http://itunes.apple.com/ca/app/keynote/id361285480?mt=8
Developer web site: http://www.apple.com/ca/ipad/from-the-app-store/
keynote.html
Internet required: Requires an Internet connection for file sharing.

What Is Keynote?

Keynote is a presentation tool that uses a slide show style to deliver content. When connected
to a projector or other display device, the presentation slides are shown on the external
display and the presenter's notes are shown on the device's display.

Figure 1 illustrates how you can select a theme from the 12 different themes available
in Keynote. A theme should be selected at the start of the presentation, as it is not easily
changed while the presentation is being developed.

Figure 1—*Select a theme*

Keynote comes with 12 different themes ranging from plain white or black background
to gradient and nine other preset styles. Within each theme are eight standard slide types
used to construct the presentation. The different slide types allow users to develop a
flexible and captivating presentation.

Ranging from blank slides to single column with or without an image or title bar, these slides cover most of the basic layouts and are customizable by adding charts, media (photos), shapes, and tables (Figure 2). Select media from the photos container. Images added to the presentation can be easily edited and manipulated.

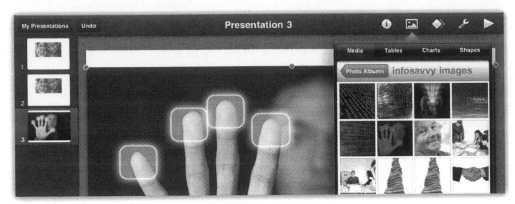

Figure 2—*Adding images*

Transitions, or the change between slides, are animated with a variety of different styles, including magic move, which allows users to create a slide and then duplicate it, repositioning the content and smoothly transitioning between the different elements in the slide.

Within the slides, users can animate the delivery and exit of content using a variety of styles. Each style can be customized to suit the requirements of users in speed and duration of delivery, selection of elements to be delivered (all at once, by bullet, and so on), and sequence. Users can customize build in (entry) and build out (exit).

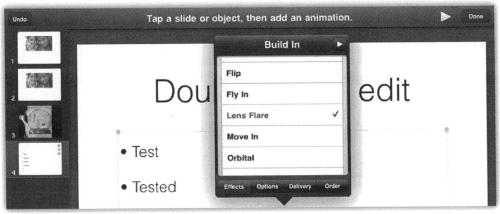

Figure 3—*Adding animation to slides*

Figure 3 shows animating the delivery of content into a slide. This process is very similar to inserting the transitions between the slides.

Media added to the presentation can be easily manipulated for size. Using the Info button, different image styles can be applied, borders can be added, and effects can be used, including transparency, shadow, and reflection. The inserted media can be moved to the front or back and rotated or flipped. There are a variety of different border styles that allow users to further customize their presentations (see Figure 4).

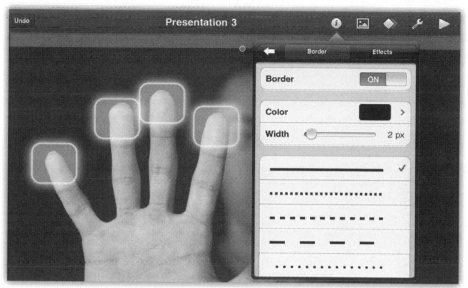

Figure 4—*Adding custom image borders*

Presentations can be shared using iDisk, email, or iTunes, as well as in either a single display from the device or an external display attached via the VGA break-out cable. The software will allow you to save the file as a Keynote file, PDF, or Microsoft PowerPoint file. PowerPoint format and Keynote files can be opened and edited in the software; however, some aspects of functionality may not be present.

Figure 5 shows how, when sharing presentations via email, users can select the format (Microsoft PowerPoint, Apple Keynote, or PDF) in which they wish to share the file.

Figure 5—*Selecting file formats*

How Can Keynote Be Used in the Classroom?

Critical to the success of any student is the ability to communicate effectively. Key to this is the ability not only to speak clearly and concisely but also to design, develop, and deliver content using a variety of tools and media. The selection and layout of the media and content is core to effectively delivering and conveying the message to a group. These are the basic elements of communication and solution fluencies.

In the classroom, presentation tools allow students to quickly and easily develop a presentation for a small group viewing the content from the device's display or for a larger group using the external display. Students can be asked to develop presentations on their own device, and then, using the ability to share the presentation in Keynote or PowerPoint formats, the presentations can be sent to other computers for display independent of whether the other computers are PCs or Macs. As users are developing the presentation, they can easily add information into the presenter's notes to script their performance. The use of presenter's notes displayed on the screen provides an excellent prompt for students as they progress through their presentation. To add presenter's notes to the presentation, select the tools menu and select Presenter's Notes (Figure 6).

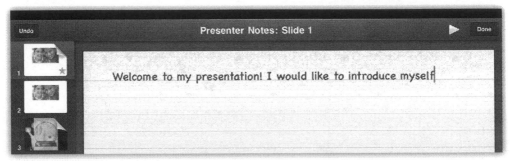

Figure 6—*Adding presenter's notes*

The ability to add graphs and charts and animate the delivery of the content is particularly useful in the sciences, social sciences, and mathematics, where learners can present their research results or findings in graphical as well as tabular form. Students asked to investigate the demographics of their age-group or the average speed of cars passing the school can graphically demonstrate their understanding of the results. The different elements of the graphs or charts can be individually animated, allowing students to speak to each element of the data as it is displayed to the audience. Figure 7 shows how inserting and animating graphs and charts allows students to talk about each element of the data series as it is presented to the group.

Figure 7—*Inserting and animating graphs*

Saving the final product as a PDF file allows users to share their presentations in a widely accepted cross-platform format.

Using the themes, students can quickly and easily construct simple photo albums or storybooks. Storybooks will lack the interactivity of buttons or the ability to embed video or audio into the product. However, the photo albums can be customized, making use of the many effects and transitions, as well as the themes, to make captivating shows.

In a math class, students can use given shapes as a quick reference point instead of having to create them on the spot. Instead of finding images of, for example, obtuse angles on Google images, students can find examples in their everyday lives, take pictures of them, and import the images into Keynote.

Keynote can also be used to develop portfolios of student visual art. By capturing and transferring pictures of their work, students can construct a dynamic visual portfolio that is easily portable and simply displayed. Users can add relevant text showing the title, date of production, and other key elements of their artwork. The small size and portability of the device means that the portfolio is available anywhere, anytime, and anyplace.

Keynote Remote

App name: Keynote Remote

Subject areas: All

Available for: iPad / iPod Touch / iPhone

Cost: $0.99

Requirements: Requires iOS 4.2 and Apple computer with Keynote.

iTunes URL: http://itunes.apple.com/us/app/keynote-remote/
id300719251?mt=8

Developer web site: http://support.apple.com/kb/HT3325

Internet required: Wi-Fi or a user-created computer-to-computer network

What Is Keynote Remote?

With Keynote Remote, users can control Keynote presentations being run from an Apple computer using their iPad, iPod Touch, or iPhone. The app requires the user to make a link between the Keynote application on the Apple computer and the Keynote Remote on the iDevice (iPad, iPod Touch, or iPhone). The Keynote Remote on the iDevice is linked to the Keynote app on the Apple computer, allowing the presenter to control the presentation from his or her iPhone, iPad, or iPod Touch (see Figure 1).

Figure 1—*Keynote Remote link*

How Does Keynote Remote Work?

Figure 2—*Add Keynote link*

Keynote Remote must be linked to control your Keynote '09 presentation from your iPhone, iPod Touch, or iPad. If you use a firewall, you may need to adjust your firewall options in order to use Keynote Remote.

The Options screen allows presenters to customize how the presentation appears on their devices. On your Mac, choose System Preferences from the Apple menu. Click Security, and then click Firewall. Click to select the "Allow all incoming connections" button. This will ensure Keynote Remote communicates with Keynote '09.

On your iPhone, choose Settings > Wi-Fi to verify you are on the same wireless network as your computer. On your computer, open your presentation in Keynote '09. Choose Preferences from the Keynote menu and select Remote, and then turn on the "Enable iPhone and iPod Touch Remotes" option. On your iPhone, open Keynote Remote, and then tap the "Link to Keynote" button. On your iPhone, select "New Keynote Link" (see Figure 2) to display a four-digit passcode.

You should now see your iPad, iPod Touch, or iPhone name in the Preferences pane on your Mac. Click the "Link" button to the right of your iPhone name. Enter the passcode displayed on your iPhone. *Note:* You may need to wait for the passcode to register—DO NOT tap Cancel!

Once the link is established, tap the Done button on your iPad, iPod Touch, or iPhone. To start your slide show, tap the Play Slideshow button on your iPhone. Once you have linked your iPhone to your computer, follow these steps to control your slide show with Keynote Remote. (*Note:* Before playing your slide show with Keynote Remote, you may want to disable incoming phone calls on your iPhone.) If it is not already open, launch your Keynote '09 presentation. On your iPhone, launch Keynote Remote. The remote allows the presenter to control the presentation. This includes moving forward and back by gestures as well as the options within the application (Figure 3).

Figure 3—*Keynote control options*

How Can Keynote Remote Be Used in the Classroom?

With Keynote Remote, students don't have to stay at the front of the classroom to present. A feature in Keynote called "Presenter Notes" allows you to basically have cue cards to help you stay on track throughout a presentation. Keynote Remote displays those presenter notes right below the current slide. The presenter's notes and the slide are clearly visible as users move from slide to slide (Figure 4).

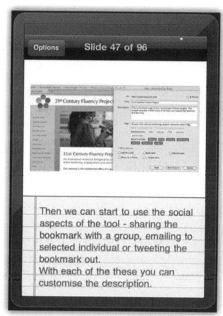

Figure 4—*Add presenter's notes*

Aside from being very cool and showing your presenter notes, all this application really does is let you change slides. Similar to using Camera Roll, just swipe left and right to go forward or backward in the slide queue. In portrait, the current slide is displayed as well as the presenter notes. In landscape, the current slide and the next slide are shown, which could be useful for talking about what's up next. One suggestion would be to use portrait and include a cue to the next slide in the presenter notes.

If you are not using Keynote as your presentation application and use Microsoft PowerPoint, there is also a clicker application, iClicker, for this tool. There is an iClicker app for both the Mac and the Windows operating systems. The iClicker app also works over a wireless network, similar to Keynote remote.

Lynkee 2 QR Barcode Reader

App name: Lynkee 2 QR Barcode Reader
Subject areas: All
Available for: iPad / iPod Touch / iPhone (4th generation)
Cost: Free
Requirements: Requires iOS 4.0 or later.
iTunes URL: http://itunes.apple.com/us/app/lynkee-2-qr-barcode-reader/ id416446101?mt=8
Developer web site: http://www.lynkware.com/eng/index.php
Internet required: Yes

about the app

What Is Lynkee 2 QR Barcode Reader?

Lynkee 2 QR uses a mobile device's embedded camera for real-time image scanning (1D barcode or 2D tags such as QR codes). By downloading and installing Lynkee, users can easily decode 1D barcodes and 2D tags on a mobile device. Users can scan tags on a number of items, for example, journals, video materials, posters, clothing, and so on, and then access additional information available on the Internet, including multimedia content such as video or audio, participate in games by sending an SMS to a predefined code, or access other features of mobile devices.

The potential for this application is endless! If students are interested in a particular topic (e.g., a newspaper article that is part of a presentation, a book they are about to report on, a monument in Washington, D.C., that is part of a social studies assignment, or an image of a billboard for class discussion in a communications class) and a 2D barcode is placed on it, they can scan the code. This code will connect them to a web site where they can find the information they are looking for and download text, images, sound, or video related to the subject directly to their mobile device.

Figure 1—Scanning options

How Does Lynkee 2 QR Barcode Reader Work?

The Lynkee app allows users to scan codes three different ways (see Figure 1). The first method is a web scan—the Lynkee browser is capable of decoding a barcode within a web page.

In Figure 2, the code opened the Committed Sardine web site. Automatically opening a site can be set as an option in the settings in the lower right corner of the app.

Figure 2—*Committed Sardine*

Once at the site, the user simply taps the www scanner in the bottom left corner of the app and it goes to wherever the user wants to go (see Figures 3 and 4).

Figure 3—*Tapping scanner icon*

Figure 4—*Open web site option*

The second option is to scan from the photo library. Tapping on file scan opens QR codes or barcodes that may have been taken as photos in the classroom, on a field trip, or even in the user's favorite place to shop (see Figure 5). When you tap on the image, it opens in the Lynkee app. As you can see in Figure 6, this barcode was to a favorite cereal.

Figure 5—*Barcode photo example*

Figure 6—*Scan result, cereal box*

The third method is to scan the QR Code with the camera of the iPad 2, iPhone, or iPod Touch 4th generation. Users simply scan the QR code or barcode and go to a web site where the teacher has made links using QR code. Teachers can create their own QR code (see Figure 7) with any reading that may be required for a class, such as the Preamble to the Constitution of the United States. The file can also be saved in the photo library (Figure 8).

Figure 7—*QR code generator*

Figure 8—*Saving in photo library*

Users can create a QR codebook of code to share via Facebook or save to their photo library. Bookmarks can "link to" text, web sites, locations, and more. The settings for the app can be seen in Figure 9, and bookmarks can be seen in Figure 10.

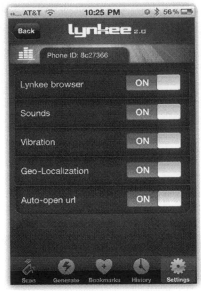

Figure 9—Settings

Figure 10—Bookmarks

How Can Lynkee 2 QR Barcode Reader Be Used in the Classroom?

Posting QR codes throughout the classroom with titles about various student works creates an interactive back-to-school night. QR codes could access student videos, projects, blogs, and many other ideas only teachers can envision. Hand out devices (iPod Touches, for instance) to parents who don't have a mobile device and show them how to read the QR code and access the materials.

Include QR codes that link to online resources, your contact information, articles, YouTube channel/playlists, your email, phone, SMS, Facebook links, Twitter, and any other resources students will need to access. Teachers can create mobile assignments as students leave the classroom by posting a QR code on the door with the title "Assignments for this Week." Students can quickly scan the QR code and have the information instantly visible on their mobile devices. They won't lose this as easily as a piece of paper! Flashcards could be created with the QR codes on the back. You could get very creative with this app and incorporate links to web sites that would provide additional information about the questions. Remember that the app also scans barcodes. Barcodes of books for students to find in a bookstore or the library could be posted. Instant surveys or quizzes can be created using a Google Docs form and creating a QR code link to that form. Students, parents, or whoever can access the form to complete the survey or quiz on the mobile device.

Students could create a guided tour of their school or a historical site, museum, or public building by researching the site, creating mobile web pages, videos, audio files, or any other type of appropriate media to provide more information, and then creating and posting the QR codes to the various locations. An interactive science project would be the talk of a science fair.

Many magazines and newspapers include QR codes inside and on their covers. Include a QR code along with the printed URL to direct parents to a mobile version of your class newsletter. Students can create weekly videos on school activities, publishing them to their school intranet or other private location, and then post QR codes that link to these updates with the notice "What's Happening in School This Week!"

Finally, students could create a cooperative learning "Code Quest" by posting QR codes at various locations. Each QR code will ask a question that will require the retrieval of an object. Once the object is found, another QR code will send students to another location to locate yet another object. A Code Quest involves teamwork, cooperation, thinking, and moving around!

Creating QR code is an easy task. Here are a few sites teachers can use to create QR code for their classrooms:

- http://www.qrstuff.com/

- http://qrcode.kaywa.com/

- http://delivr.com/qr-code-generator

Note Taker HD

App name: Note Taker HD
Subject areas: All
Available for: iPad 1 and 2
Cost: $4.99
Requirements: Requires iOS 3.2 or later.
iTunes URL: http://itunes.apple.com/ca/app/note-taker-hd/id366572045?mt=8
Developer web site: http://www.softwaregarden.com/products/notetakerhd/
Internet required: No

What Is Note Taker HD?

Note Taker HD is an application for writing and organizing notes and diagrams. This powerful app allows users to enter text via stylus (Figure 1) or screen keyboard (Figure 2). It can be used in almost any classroom situation.

Figure 1—Handwriting entry box

Figure 2—Text entry keyboard

How Does Note Taker HD Work?

As a tool, Note Taker HD allows students to take notes, develop ideas, draw, create diagrams, and even construct graphs. The pages the students create can be grouped or ordered into "sheets." Sheets and pages can be reopened, edited, and shared at any time in the future. They can be shared as PDF documents or opened in sharing archive applications such as Evernote and Dropbox. Note Taker HD also supports printing.

A powerful feature of Note Taker HD is its ability to embed images and scalable adaptable shapes and objects such as graphs into the pages (Figure 3). These can be easily manipulated. Students using the iPad 2 are able to use the camera in the device to add images.

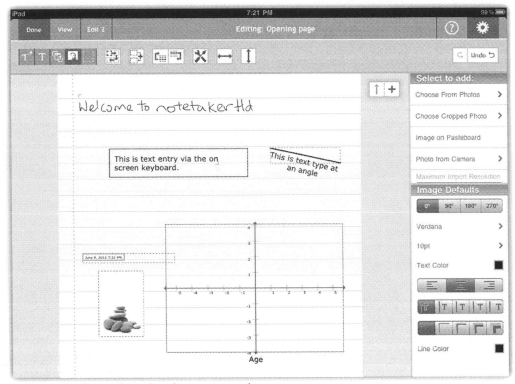

Figure 3—*Page with graph and images inserted*

How Can Note Taker HD Be Used in the Classroom?

In the classroom, Note Taker HD allows students to take notes easily. They have the option of using the keyboard or entering the notes in handwritten form. Handwritten notes are entered in a magnified text entry box at the bottom of the page (see Figure 1). This entry space is scaled so the text is written in a large form but appears at an appropriate size on the page. Students can use their fingers to enter text, but using a stylus, which must be purchased at additional cost, is much more accurate.

The shapes and auto text allow students to add date and time stamps to their notes, which allows for continuity of work. They can add shapes and annotate diagrams they have drawn, and they can also embed images and annotate and label them. This feature has obvious applications in the classroom; a student can be provided with a map, diagram, or image and then asked to annotate it, labeling key parts and so forth. The finished diagram can be exported as a PDF file and shared with the student's peers or submitted to the teacher using email, Evernote, or Dropbox.

One of the most exciting features of Note Taker HD is the graphing tool, which has immediate application to the mathematics, science, and humanities classrooms. Students are able to add single-quadrant and four-quadrant line graphs, pie charts, 3D bar graphs, circle/polar graphs, and tables to their pages. The axis can be labeled and scaled so graphs of almost any style or shape can be created, plotted, and annotated. By using a template, the students are able to create accurate graphs. They can increase the frequency of the grid, allowing very precise graphs to be plotted. There is also a straight-line plotting tool that allows the students to add a straight line or line of best fit to their graphs.

A wide variety of other shapes and objects are available that make Note Taker HD a useful tool in any classroom (Figure 4). These include the musical templates—musical staff lines, guitar tablature, and chords charts—that make Note Taker HD a useful tool for music notation and simple composition. The flowchart tool set is useful in the computer science and information technology classroom, as students are able to construct process flowcharts and visualize computer programs and processes.

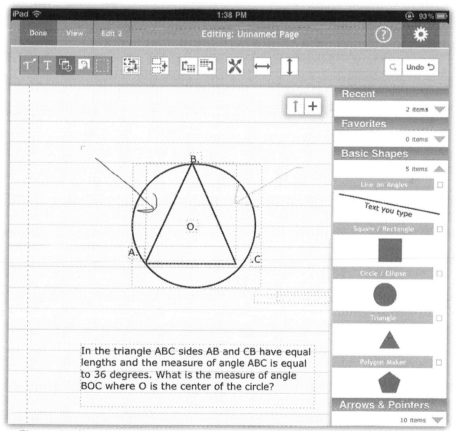

Figure 4—*Shapes and templates*

In many ways, Note Taker HD is a replacement for traditional pen and paper, as it combines the flexibility of stylus-based text entry and drawing with the structure of a variety of templates, objects, and shapes. A wide range of pens, nibs, and colors are available for students to use (Figure 5). The highlighter tools are useful when students revise and reflect on their class notes and personal research.

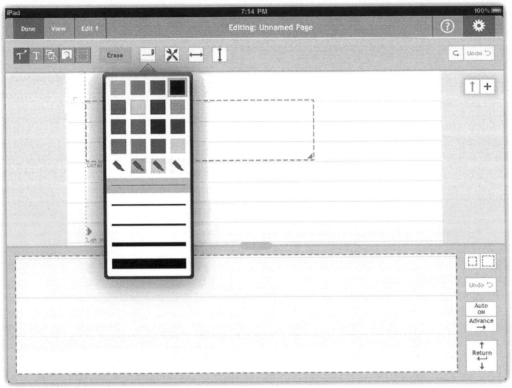

Figure 5—*Color palette*

Numbers

App name: Numbers
Subject areas: All
Available for: iPad / iPod Touch / iPhone
Cost: $9.99
Requirements: Requires iOS 4.2.8 or later.
iTunes URL: http://www.apple.com/ipad/from-the-app-store/numbers.html
Developer web site: http://www.apple.com/au/ipad/features/numbers.html
Internet required: Not for operation, but only to share files by email or iDisk

What Is Numbers?

Numbers is a data processing tool and spreadsheet application. This tool enables users to enter and process data in a variety of forms and display these as tables, charts, and so on. Applicable in all subject areas, Numbers allows the organization and processing of raw facts and figures (data) into processed information.

How Does Numbers Work?

Numbers is a member of the iWorks family of productivity tools produced by Apple and is compatible with the full versions of the product created for Apple computers by exporting spreadsheets in Numbers format. The completed spreadsheets can also be exported in Microsoft Excel XLS format or as PDFs (see Figure 1).

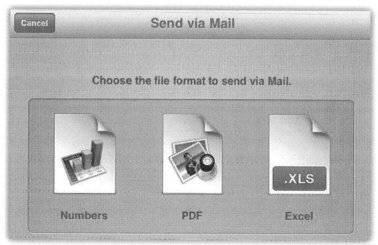

Figure 1—*Spreadsheet formats*

Numbers has 16 chart and graph templates for users to select from, ranging from personal budgets to class attendance rosters (see Figure 2).

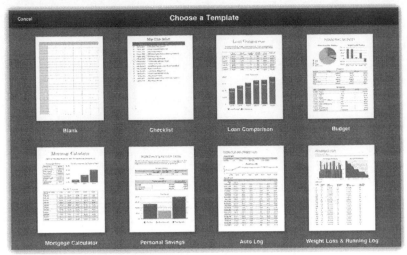

Figure 2*—Numbers templates*

The range of available templates makes developing new sheets with high functionality easy. The sheets can be easily adapted to meet the needs of users or to develop an understanding of the processes used to create the product.

When opening the app, users are presented with a straightforward 10-tab tutorial (see Figure 3) that leads them through entry of data, use of templates, formatting, and use of forms. From here, is it easy to construct their own initial spreadsheets. The tutorial is an easy guide to using most of the basic features of Numbers.

Figure 3*—Spreadsheet creation wizard*

The product supports multiple sheets within a document and a wide variety of charts and graphs. The process of selecting the ranges of cells to use is fast and easy and leads to quick development of visual representations of the information. The ability to go into full-screen mode allows the product to be used for presenting the data as well.

Setting up columns and formatting them into data types is also straightforward and allows users to lay out their spreadsheets in the correct format before data is entered. The data entry method is specific for the format of the cell, making entry quick and efficient. From the data entry pane, users can move across the record or down to the next record. Data types available to use are

- Number

- Currency

- Percentage

- Date and time

- Duration

- Check box

- Star ratings

- Text

The ability to easily enter check boxes and star ratings and then include these in calculations is useful and allows users to collect opinions in a simple and easy manner. Formatting the selected range of cells to the date and time format is required (Figure 4).

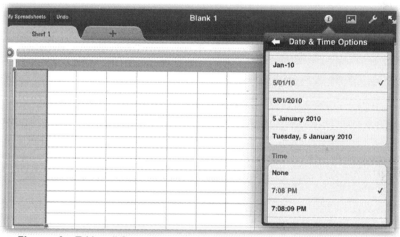

Figure 4—*Table cell formatting*

The range of available functions is broad, with more than 250 available in the product. This is limited compared with a fully featured spreadsheet product such as iWorks Numbers, Microsoft Excel, or Open Office Calc, but for the average user it should be sufficient.

Users can also develop simple data entry forms that link to a collecting spreadsheet. This allows users to develop a form containing only the information fields and to have the information collected in this form rather than directly into the spreadsheet. Both this and the flexibility of the device make data collection in the field easy and efficient.

An example of the form from the tutorial is illustrated in Figure 5 on the following page. This form links to a spreadsheet and enters the data directly into the cells within each record.

Figure 5—*Numbers tutorial form*

How Can Numbers Be Used in the Classroom?

The uses of the basic spreadsheet functions in the classroom are broad. Whether students use templates such as the weight loss and running log, team organization, or stats lab or develop spreadsheets of their own, this tool is useful. The ability to immediately see data being entered on a graph allows users to consider the trends and undertake higher-order thinking by analyzing and eventually evaluating the processed data or information. The ability to visualize the data quickly and then easily modify the form of data visualization by changing the graph is a powerful tool in developing depth and clarity in understanding.

When the basic spreadsheet functions are linked to the use of data collection forms, the capacity and usefulness of the tool increases again.

For example, in biology, students are asked to survey the diversity and abundance of life using a series of quadrants along a transecting line through a rocky platform on the seashore. The range of species students will encounter is known and a data entry form is developed for sampling at each point down the transect line. As students proceed down the line and enter the data, they can see the changes in relative abundance and the impact of zonation.

In social sciences, students could be sampling the popularity of food sold at the school canteen or cafeteria. A form could be developed that asks students to give a star rating on the different foods, and then collects suggestions in a text field for alternatives that they would like to see provided. Since the data are entered into a form rather than directly into the spreadsheet, the person being sampled is unlikely to be influenced by the previous responses. The ability to set up graphs and charts when laying out the spreadsheet means that data collected can be quickly examined and reported.

The design aspect of all of these examples is critical. The well-designed product shows higher-order thinking and an understanding of the variable. It also shows a good understanding of the goals and objectives of the task. These are critical aspects of solution fluency.

In language arts and media, students can use the spreadsheet and its different data fields to create a storyboard for a video they are making or to analyze the composition and structure of a short film being studied. They can enter the information directly into the spreadsheet or develop a form to allow them to analyze each scene for the following characteristics:

- Act and scene number
- Duration
- Participants
- Action
- Camera angle
- Effects
- Location
- Dialogue

This provides a detailed record of the scenes, and when linked with the ability to order and sort the data, students are able to arrange their analysis into sequence even if the discussion of the scenes was nonsequential.

Pages

App name: Pages
Subject areas: All
Available for: iPad / iPod Touch / iPhone
Cost: $9.99
Requirements: Requires iOS 4.2.8 or later.
iTunes URL: http://itunes.apple.com/ca/app/pages/id361309726?mt=8
Developers web site: http://www.apple.com/au/ipad/features/pages.html
Internet required: Not for operation, but for sharing files via email or iDisk

What Is Pages?

Pages is a core application for the classroom toolkit. A powerful word processor, Pages allows users to create, edit, and print documents from templates or a blank page. Like its big brother on Apple computers, Pages is also a desktop publishing tool. This tool is useful across the curricula and throughout all levels of the school.

How Does Pages Work?

This is one of the iWorks series of productivity tools available for the iPad. These other members of the suite of tools (each of which can be individually purchased or installed) are also available:

- *Numbers:* spreadsheet and data processing tool (purchased product)

- *Keynote:* presentation tool (purchased product)

- *Mobile Me Gallery:* free utility that allows you to upload photographs to your Mobile Me account (free but requires a Mobile Me account)

- *Mobile Me iDisk:* allows easy one-click access to your Mobile Me account (free but requires a Mobile Me account)

  The word processor has all of the major functions including

- *Basic editing and formatting tools:* bold, italic, underline, alignment indent and tab, bullet points, columns, color, and font selection

- *Styles:* headings, subheadings, title, body, label, bullet, header, footer, footnote, and so on

- *Graphics:* Insert tables, charts, and graphs; media (video and images); shapes; lists (unordered with bullets or images or ordered with numbers or letters)

Additionally, Pages comes with 16 different templates that can be selected when starting a new document (Figure 1).

Figure 1—*New/duplicate document*

The document setup function allows users to adjust the margins, page width and height, and header and footer dimensions in a quirky "blueprint" style page (Figure 2).

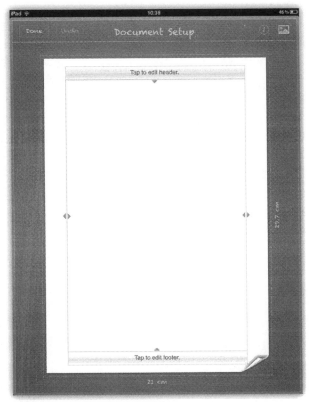

Figure 2—*Document setup*

The templates (Figure 3) are both basic word processing and desktop publishing. They include

- Word processing templates: letter, proposal, resume, visual report, term paper, recipe, and syllabus

- Desktop publishing templates: poster, party invite, thank-you card, and flyer.

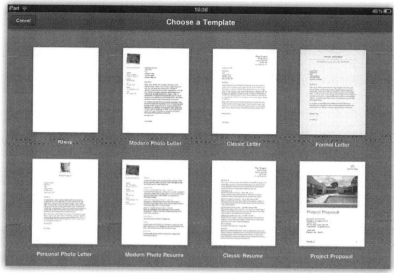

Figure 3—*Template choices*

Special characters can be accessed via the iPad keyboard by pressing and holding the character key and sliding your finger to select the appropriate character. This feature continues into the second and third levels of the keyboard. For example, holding the $ key down will bring up a variety of currency symbols to be inserted (Figure 4).

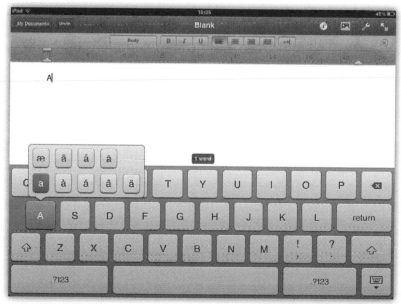

Figure 4—*Special characters*

Pages allows users to create and open documents in Pages '09 format and Microsoft Word format. As content is entered into the document, it is automatically saved, so closing the document does not loose any entered information. Further, the undo feature of the word processor operates between opening and closing the document. Undos from the previous editing session are available in the new session. When saving the document to be exported, users can save it in three different file formats depending on the purpose of the export and its destination. The three formats are

- Microsoft Word document
- iWorks Pages '09
- PDF format (portable document format)

Documents can be printed from an installed printer, or they can be shared using

- email
- iDisk
- iTunes sharing
- WEBDAV

How Can Pages Be Used in the Classroom?

As a classroom tool, the Pages word processor is applicable across all subject areas and across most age-groups. Access to features and tool sets is via four buttons on the tool bar. While they are clearly visible, they are not particularly intuitive. However, once selected, the tools within the menus are easy to use and apply (Figure 5).

Figure 5—*Tools access*

The working space for entering text is limited by the onscreen keyboard but is still usable and functional. Switching between portrait and landscape alignment of the iPad will increase or decrease the area of the screen available and inversely decrease or increase the size of the keyboard (see Figures 6 and 7).

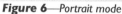

Figure 6—*Portrait mode*   **Figure 7**—*Landscape mode*

The presentation mode removes the tool bars and hides the keyboard, allowing users to display their products. This makes an effective tool for students presenting their work to a small group or the teacher. For presentation to a wider group via a projector or a computer monitor, a third-party application, such as a projector, allows students to utilize a larger viewing area.

The templates allow users to select a basic format and layout and then modify it to suit their needs and requirements (see Figure 8). More templates are available as a third-party application sold separately called Templates for Pages, which adds 23 additional templates.

Figure 8—*Sample poster project*

The portable nature of the iPad allows users to develop their reports and content when and where the need arises. For example, a teacher may prepare a worksheet for a field trip or experiment. The document could have questions and requirements students must complete as they participate in the activity. The teacher could either preload the material onto the devices using iTunes or email the students the document in a suitable format. As the students undertake the experience, they can add answers, observations, and comments. Students can then either submit the document to the teacher via email or upload it to a shared space on iDisk. Users taking photographs can upload them to the Mobile Me gallery and then download them into the product, or take them directly from the in-built cameras on the second generation iPad.

Using additional templates from the Inspiration for iPad app ($1.99, requires iOS 4.2 or later), students can create a press release with a persuasive argument for their English language arts class. For an oral communications project, students could write and then read their resume. The class could then decide whether they would hire this person based on the wording and design of the resume.

Skype

App name: Skype
Subject areas: All
Available for: iPad / iPod Touch / iPhone
Cost: Free
Requirements: Requires iOS 3.0 or later; video calling requires iOS 4 or above.
iTunes URL: http://itunes.apple.com/us/app/skype/id304878510?mt=8
Developer web site: http://www.skype.com/intl/en/welcomeback/?intcmp=wlogo
Internet required: Yes—Skype accounts must be set up on a computer prior to signing in on the mobile device.

What Is Skype?

Skype is an application for teachers to open up their classroom and their students to a world way beyond their campus. With Skype, students can learn from and with other students, connect with other cultures, and expand their knowledge. Skype provides access to voice and video communication free in most cases.

Skype provides an easy, inexpensive way for students and teachers to communicate with people anywhere. Skype opens the door to a wide range of activities that can improve engagement and comprehension. With Skype, learning becomes much more authentic because it expands beyond the walls of the classroom. Skype also allows teachers and students to engage in synchronous communication.

How Does Skype Work?

Users download the free app from iTunes. The Skype account will have to be set up first on a computer. Once logged in (Figure 1), the user will see his or her contacts. Contacts will show up on a green cloud with a white check box next to each contact's name.

Figure 1—*Skype login screen*

The Skype contacts with a phone number attached to their information will have a telephone by their name (Figure 2).

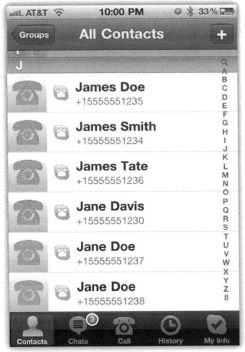

Figure 2—Contacts list

Contacts can be chosen by any of the criteria listed in Figure 3. At the bottom of the Skype home screen, users can select all contacts, open chats, or call landlines or cell phones with Skype credit. Texting is also allowed with this feature.

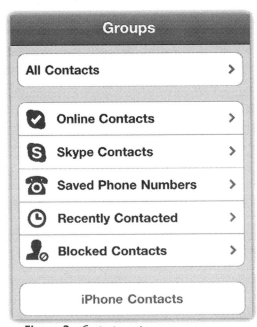

Figure 3—Contact groups

Call history and user info are the other two options from the home screen. With the iOS devices with cameras, a new picture can be added to the profile at any time (Figure 4).

Figure 4—*Adding a photo*

To start Skype calls, choose someone from all contacts or one of the filtered choices. In Figure 5, the contact and the contact's status is shown.

Figure 5—*Skype contact status*

Clicking on Call shows on the recipient's screen where he or she can either answer or decline the call. If you are using an iPad 2, iPhone 4, or iPod Touch 4th generation, there is an option to make a video call and show or view with either the front or back camera.

The Skype app is only an iPhone or iPod Touch app in the iTunes store, so click on the 2x in the bottom right corner of the iPad. Using Skype with a Skype credit account, you can make group calls from a computer to several devices, including cell phones and landlines (Figure 6).

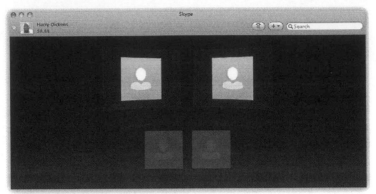

Figure 6—*Calling multiple contacts*

How Can Skype Be Used in the Classroom?

Students can travel from their classroom to other countries, visit with authors in the library or classroom, visit professionals in a career education classroom, spend time with a visual or musical artist in the art classroom or music room, and more. Inexpensive field trips can be made, and afterschool tutoring can be done with Skype. With the iPad 2, iPod Touch 4th generation, or iPhone, video calls can be made to others on their "iDevices" (Figure 7) .

Figure 7—*Call to external device*

Students can practice their presentation skills with others and receive immediate feedback. They could practice their interview skills with a human resource office in the careers the students plan to pursue. There are many web sites suggesting ways Skype can be used in the classroom. Video calls can be received with the iPad, iPhone 3Gs, or iPod Touch 3rd generation.

- Interview authors, astronauts, and other amazing individuals from around the world.

- Collaborate with classrooms, businesses, and more in multidisciplinary projects.

- Explore a volcano, rainforest, or history museum in virtual field trips with experts in the field or even share your field trip experiences with others.

- Practice conversational foreign languages with native speakers.

- Provide additional support for students needing extra attention or unable to come to class.

- Invite a guest lecturer drawn from leading educators and experts anywhere in the world.

- Explore foreign cultures firsthand with classroom-to-classroom video conferencing.

- Broadcast a performance or project to parents and families unable to make it to school.

- Access and share professional development opportunities with educators on the go.

- Collaborate with innovative educators to plan units, lessons, and more.

Advanced Uses

The Skype in the Classroom site (http://education.skype.com) and also GlobalSchoolNet.org (www.globalschoolnet.org/) are great places to find teachers who share the mission of expanding 21st-century learning and improving performance through content-driven collaboration.

- *Skype in the Classroom Ning* is for teachers interested in using Skype to connect with other teachers for idea sharing and classroom video conferencing (http://maculspace. ning.com/group/skypeintheclassroom).

- *The Mixxer* is a free educational community for language exchanges via Skype (http:// www.language-exchanges.org/).

- *Meet the Author Network* connects you with numerous authors willing to enter your library or classroom for 10- to 15-minute Skype sessions for free. You can also set up longer interviews for a fee (http://skypeanauthor.wetpaint.com/).

Global Skype Projects

- *Global School Network* engages classrooms worldwide in meaningful project-based learning exchanges to develop science, math, and literacy skills and foster collaboration, global citizenship, and multicultural understandings (http://www.globalschoolnet.org/).

- *Taking It Global* is an online community of global educators with the goal of making a difference in the world (http://www.tigweb.org/).

- *Around the World With 80 Schools,* introduced on the Langwitches blog, challenges teachers to connect with 80 different schools via Skype in order to circle the globe once (http://langwitches.org/blog/2009/01/03/around-the-world-with-80-schools/).

Skype in Education Directories

Connect with other educators looking for video conferencing classroom partnerships at these directories:

- *Skype in Schools Directory* (http://skypeinschools.pbworks.com/w/page/11008318/FrontPage)

- *Eduskypers Phonebook* (http://skypeintheclassroom.wordpress.com/2008/10/31/lets-build-a-community/#comments)

TED

App name: TED
Subject areas: All
Available for: iPad 1 and 2
Cost: Free
Requirements: Requires iOS 3.2 or later.
iTunes URL: http://itunes.apple.com/ca/app/ted-mobile/id303299045?mt=8
Developer web site: http://www.ted.com
Internet required: Yes, but videos can be downloaded for off-line viewing.

What Is TED?

TED stands for Technology, Entertainment, and Design (Figure 1). TED is a series of annual conferences bringing together the most interesting and challenging speakers. The app allows users to access and view videos from the archive of TED Talks, which can then be saved for off-line viewing.

Figure 1—TED: Technology, Entertainment, and Design

How Does TED Work?

At the various TED events around the world, speakers are recorded presenting, and then these videos are uploaded to the TED web site (http://www.ted.com) and made available for download and viewing via the TED application on the iPad 1 and 2.

The application displays the most recent videos and featured talks. Clicking on these will open an information page with key information about the talk and the speaker, advice on what to watch next, and related topics. Once the video starts playing, users have the ability to save the talk for off-line viewing.

Figure 2—*Featured videos*

The Features page of TED shows the most current or featured Ted videos (Figure 2). The application boasts a number of other features including themes and tags, which allow users to select related videos to view.

The search tool will search the entire archive for videos that match the search terms. A fun feature of the application is the Inspire Me button (Figure 3), which allows users to select from a variety of categories, including these:

- Courageous
- Funny
- Persuasive
- Ingenious
- Jaw-dropping

Users can select the time frame they have available to watch the video (Figure 4). The app will then either show a playlist or play a selection. The Inspire Me feature selects videos automatically based on the category and length of time available.

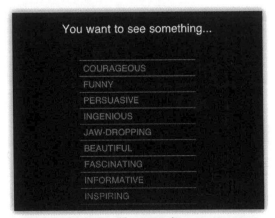

Figure 3—*Inspire Me options list*

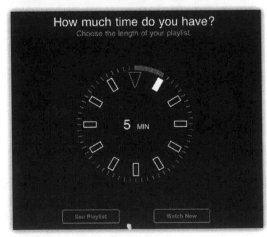

Figure 4—*Time frame options*

How Can TED Be Used in the Classroom?

The TED videos are an amazing resource for students. The world's best speakers, talking about current topics, new inventions, and current issues, are all available using this archive of videos. The classic Sir Ken Robinson video, "Schools Kill Creativity," is a great example of how this tool can be used to challenge, promote, and provoke discussion and debate. This selection can be set as a required "reading." Staff can view it and then come together as a reading circle to discuss their opinions and thoughts on this challenging video.

The TED videos can also be used with senior classes. Using the Tags (see Figure 5), teachers can quickly find videos that are of benefit to the learning outcomes of their students.

Figure 5—*TED Tags*

The Tags allow users to quickly refine and reduce searches for suitable videos. A search of the tag "biology" reveals 55 videos that are tagged with this term. Teachers then select the videos by refining the Tag search and can view them to check their suitability to their learning outcomes and objectives. Students are then directed to the video either via the TED application on the iPad or by using the iPad 2's video mirroring to share the video with the class. Using this tool, students can be brought up-to-date with the latest developments or be challenged to debate the importance, ethics, or fairness of the theme of the video.

TED's global perspective provides interesting cultural insights. TED Events are hosted around the world and often feature amazing presenters speaking about incredible topics that would normally never be available. These talks enhance global awareness and global digital citizenship. The tag for talks on the topic "Biology" is just one example (shown in Figure 6 on the following page).

Figure 6—*Biology tag*

Figure 7—*All Themes tag*

TED talks can inspire kids about what they may want to do in the future. There are TED talks about becoming entrepreneurs. Career choices could be influenced by watching a TED Talk from the What's Next in Tech theme. Users can search by themes (see Figure 7). These themes are grouped by topics, including

- *A Greener Future?*

- *What's Next in Tech*

- *Women Reshaping the World*

- *The Rise of Collaboration*

So many TED talks can be used to inspire students. The micro-sculpture talk by Willard Wigan would be an inspiring topic for a sculpture class. The micro-sculptures he has created are hold-your-breath amazing (see Figure 8).

Figure 8—*Art-on-Needlehead*

In a science class, students could explore how he creates his art using a microfiber he pulls out of the air, or a grain of sand. Biology students could explore how he slows his heartbeat so he can work between the beats.

Teleprompt+

App name: Teleprompt+
Subject areas: All
Available for: iPad 1 and 2
Cost: $14.99
Requirements: Requires iOS 3.2 or later.
iTunes URL: http://itunes.apple.com/us/app/teleprompt-for-ipad/id364903926?mt=8
Developer web site: http://www.bombingbrain.com/
Internet required: Yes, for remote interface and downloading files online

What Is Teleprompt+?

A teleprompter is a commonly used device in video production. It provides broadcasters with an electronic display of their lines or script on a monitor, often scrolling the text as the broadcaster speaks. The Teleprompt+ app allows users to create video or audio speeches. This is a useful tool in the television studios of many middle and high schools and can be used in any classroom where students are performing a speech. For podcasting, Teleprompter+ is a better alternative to using cue cards because you can seamlessly read an entire segment by yourself, eliminating the need for an extra person.

The Teleprompt+ application allows you to write your speaking scripts directly in the Teleprompt+ app itself using the built-in text editor, or by copying/pasting from Mail, Pages, or any other iPad app. The app integration with Google docs and Dropbox allows for a quick retrieval of text from either online storage site.

How Does Teleprompt+ Work?

When the app is opened, the options are to open practice scripts, including the Gettysburg Address by Abraham Lincoln and the "I Have a Dream" speech by Dr. Martin Luther King Jr. (see Figure 1). The plus symbol opens the script box and users can write directly into the application.

Figure 1—Script selections

The import feature allows text files only to be imported into the app (see Figure 2).

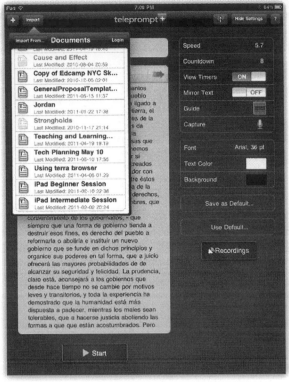

Figure 2—*Text import*

When users click on the antenna icon, the application looks for the remote control app, which can be run from another iPad, iPhone, or iPod Touch. When the screen is clicked, the text begins playing and the play button at the bottom of the screen allows users to track their progress using the integrated timer display (estimate, actual, and remaining time). Users can pause, play, and adjust playback speed during prompting (see Figure 3).

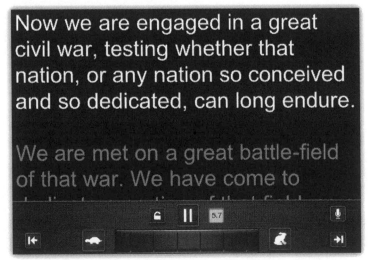

Figure 3—*Adjust during playback*

In the settings, users can customize the appearance and playback settings per script. The options are

- Scrolling speed

- Start countdown

- Timer display

- Add a guide for text reading

- Capture audio (iPad first generation)

- Font type

- Font size

- Text and background color

The iPad 2 additional features include video recording. The front camera can be used for direct prompting and informal on-the-go recording sessions. The rear HD camera can be used to demonstrate product or show a subject while reading from the prompter and recording audio. Multiple takes can be recorded and video can be exported using iTunes file sharing. Video can be exported to Photo Library to send via email, post to YouTube, or edit in iMovie or ReelDirector. The app also supports AirPlay—users can stream recorded videos right from Teleprompt+ to AppleTV. Users can pinch, move, or hide the video window to set up the prompter the way they like it.

How Can Teleprompt+ Be Used in the Classroom?

Most would think the Teleprompt+ app would be used in a television production classroom. But why not in a marketing, English, social studies, science, drama, or oral communication classroom? In marketing, creating a radio or television commercial with this app is versatile as the teleprompter makes recording a commercial portable. In some schools, students would recite the morning announcements using Teleprompter+, so there would be no getting lost on the page. A better flow of the text would happen as well, especially using the guides to fix the student's eye position while they read from the application. Students can create documents in Google Docs or Dropbox to be uploaded into the program (see Figure 4).

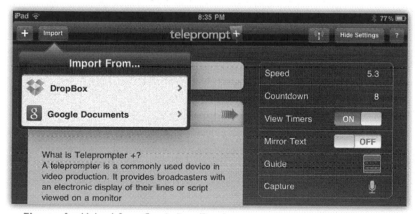

Figure 4—*Upload from Google Docs/Dropbox*

Advanced Uses

The Teleprompt+ app can easily be used for cross-curricular activities. Students could create commercials for an item to market for a marketing class. They would create the text for the commercial in an English or foreign language class using Pages or another iPad word processor. They could create the product as a science project. Last, but not least, they could add student-created music (fine arts) from Garage Band, and the final poduction could be created in an oral communication class or drama class. Doing a project in this manner, students will get an understanding of how all of their subjects can interact and are not meant to be stand-alone courses.

Students could use the Dragon Dictation app for book talks and paste their thoughts into the Teleprompter+ app, record the audio, and share the result with classmates or the teacher. The app could be used in a foreign language class to practice reading a script of a play or any class assignment (see Figure 5). The text shown in this example is taken from the Declaration of Independence, written in Spanish.

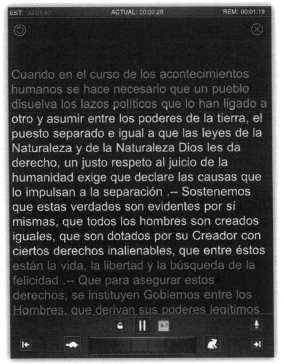

Figure 5—*Language study example*

Whiteboard HD

about the app

App name: Whiteboard HD
Subject areas: All
Available for: iPad
Cost: $4.99
Requirements: VGA adapter for projection; iOS 3.2 or later.
iTunes URL: http://itunes.apple.com/us/app/whiteboard-hd/id383779666?mt=8
Developer web site: www.avicisoftware.com/whiteboard
Internet required: Not for use; only to transfer files to Box.net or Dropbox

What Is Whiteboard HD?

Whiteboard HD is an app that mimics many of the basic features of an interactive whiteboard. This app can be used to prepare a presentation and allows users to add text, shapes, images, and freehand drawings while projecting onto a screen or monitor. The application is mirrored on the screen.

Whiteboard HD uses touch recognition to insert pictures and shapes or connect lines and text (Figure 1).

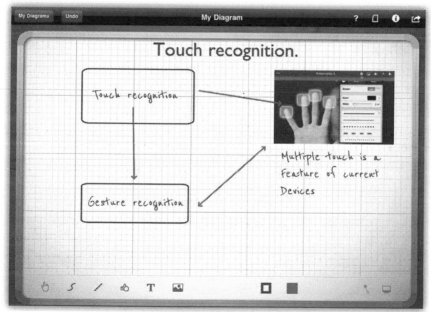

Figure 1—Whiteboard's touch recognition feature

Whiteboard HD has a useful selection of symbols that lend themselves well to mathematical formulas, making this a flexible presentation tool across all subject areas.

The Whiteboard HD toolbar (Figure 2) has the basic tool set but also includes fill and border tools, a laser pointer, and a monitor scan tool. This is the basic tool set for developing diagrams:

- *Selection tool*—This allows the teacher or student to select and manipulate the objects.

- *Freehand drawing tool*—You can create free-form drawings by dragging your finger.

- *Straight-line drawing tool*—A useful feature of this tool is its ability to change the line starting and ending styles, allowing users to insert arrows and the like.

- *Shapes tool*—A wide selection of different shapes are available, and these are manipulated by using two fingers to resize, reposition, and rotate.

- *Text tool*—This tool allows users to add text but extends the number of available keyboards to include mathematical symbols and the Greek alphabet, ideal for mathematics.

- *Images tool*—Users can add images from a range of sources including Dropbox.

Figure 2—*Whiteboard HD toolbar*

The monitor scan option scans for attached devices and allows presenters to connect to these to present their Whiteboards. The finished Whiteboards can be shared via a range of tools and in a number of different formats.

Files can be exported to the following:

- email

- Dropbox

- Box.net

- My pictures

Format export options (Figure 3) include

- Image with transparency

- Image with white background

- PDF file

- Whiteboard file

Figure 3—*Export options*

How Can Whiteboard HD Be Used in the Classroom?

Whiteboard HD provides a way of presenting to and developing diagrams for the class. Making use of existing technology, such as projectors and monitors, teachers or students can quickly share previously developed Whiteboards or create new ones as they present. This capability lends itself to collaborative interactions. The simple tool set allows the presenter to quickly create a Whiteboard and alter it as required from anywhere in the classroom or beyond.

The extensive keyboard of mathematical symbols and the Greek alphabet (Figure 4) make this a powerful tool for teachers and students of math alike. The presented Whiteboards can easily include mathematical formulas and equations that would be time-consuming to draw by hand. The symbols keyboard makes adding mathematical symbols and letters of the Greek alphabet simple.

Figure 4—*Special characters keyboard*

Whiteboard also allows users to develop simple flowcharts using a variety of shapes and different line start and end points. The shapes are simple and do not include the more specialized shapes that would be useful for such applications as information technology and computing flowcharts.

Inserting a shape is straightforward and allows for easy construction of flowcharts and other diagrams (Figure 5).

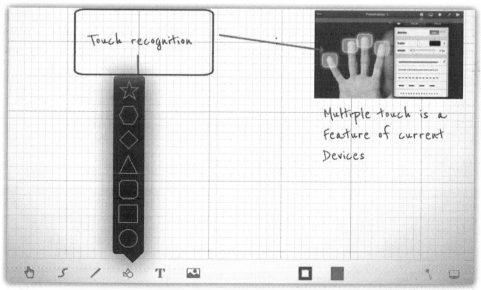

Figure 5—*Inserting symbols*

Lines can be modified by adding start and end styles. The Inspector tool allows users to modify color, thickness, style position, layers, and so on (Figure 6).

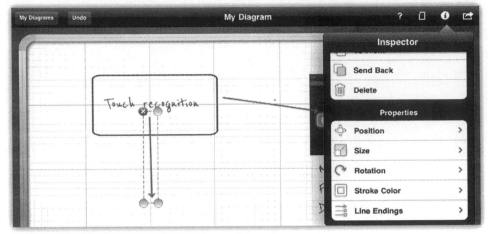

Figure 6—*The Inspector tool*

Civics or social studies students could look at a current election and create a real-time visual to see who is running. Using the Whiteboard HD as an interactive board, students could learn about the electoral college and explore different election scenarios (Figures 7 and 8).

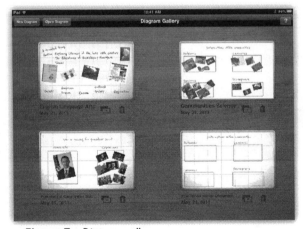

Figure 7—*Diagram gallery*

Figure 8—*Presidential candidates whiteboard*

For an English language arts class, this app can allow students to present their material in a non-linear way, allowing crosscurricular topics and studies to be explored more deeply (see Figure 9).

Figure 9—*Cross-curricular study in langauge arts*

Wikihood/ Wikihood Plus

App name: Wikihood Plus for iPad / Wikihood for iPad

Subject areas: State history, world history, U.S. history, geography

Available for: iPad / iPod Touch / iPhone

Cost: $6.99 for iPad and iPad 2 / Free for iPhone and iPod Touch

Requirements: Requires iOS 4.2 or later.

iTunes URL: http://itunes.apple.com/us/app/wikihood-plus-for-ipad/id378359093?mt=8

Developer web site: http://www.wikihood.com/Start.html

Internet required: Yes

What Is Wikihood?

Wikihood Plus for iPad allows users to see sights around them or other places around the world (Figure 1). Students can find historical places, such as museums and castles, and also famous persons connected with these places or historical battles that occurred at them.

***Figure 1**—Wikihood historical search*

How Does Wikihood Work?

Wikihood combines your geographic location with Wikipedia data to show you important sites in your area, what spots others have found interesting, historical events that took place nearby, and famous people who have been linked to your area (Figures 2, 3, and 4).

How Can Wikihood Be Used in the Classroom?

Students can pinpoint historical points of interest, and they can also discover famous individuals associated with these locations, as well as important historical events that occurred there.

Figure 2—*Important sites (area search)*

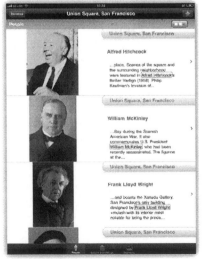

Figure 3—*Historical connections*

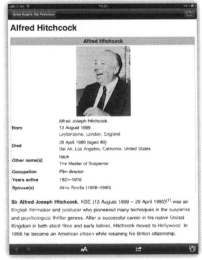

Figure 4—*Alfred Hitchcock bio*

Advanced Uses

When you first load Wikihood, either choose to manually enter a location or allow the app to automatically access your geographic location by enabling location services (Figure 5).

Figure 5—*Location search*

Within seconds of determining your location, Wikihood loads an expandable list of popular sites and information for that area, along with photos (Figure 6).

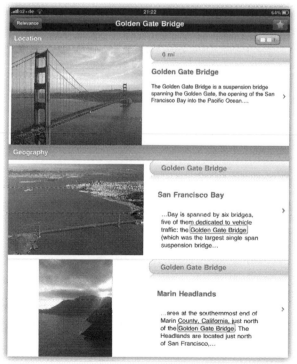

Figure 6—*Popular site information*

Using the navigation bar at the bottom of the app, you can filter listings by sorting through nearest distance and highest relevance based on what users have rated or commented on (Figures 7).

Figure 7—*Sorting by relevance*

You can also view landmarks in a Google Map view with pushpin markers at all points of interest in your locale (Figure 8).

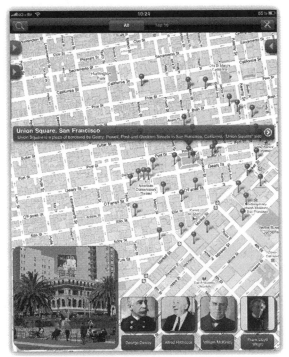

Figure 8—*Landmark locations*

To find more details, simply click through each item and Wikihood pulls in more and more Wikipedia information for you to digest. Wikihood has everything you could possibly want to extend its usage. The app contains font controls, email forwarding, an option to view in Safari, photo viewing, and a feature that provides directions to a landmark. Students can analyze information about places and the environment using this app, and they can also use Google's views of the location, which include a simple map, a satellite map, and a hybrid of these.

In an art class, seeing the Metropolitan Museum of Art would allow for a discussion about art, textures, and architecture (see Figures 9, 10, and 11).

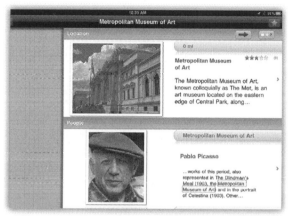

Figure 9—*Metropolitan museum search*

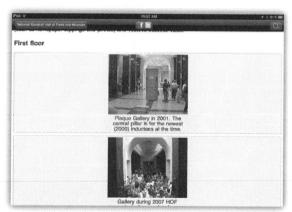

Figure 10—*Images by floor*

Figure 11—*Interior view of museum, first floor*

In a history class, students could use the Baseball Hall of Fame and Museum to begin studying Jackie Robinson, the first African American player in the major leagues, and the history of race and sports (see Figures 12, 13, and 14).

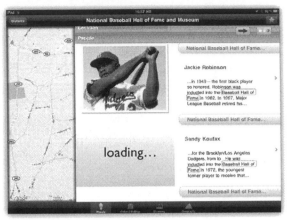

Figure 12—*Baseball Hall of Fame search*

Figure 13—*Images by floor*

Figure 14—*The First Class display*

Section 3

Specialty APPS

Algebra Touch

App name: Algebra Touch
Subject areas: Mathematics
Available for: iPad / iPod Touch / iPhone
Cost: $1.99
Requirements: Requires iOS 4.0 or later.
iTunes URL: http://itunes.apple.com/us/app/algebra-touch/id384354262?mt=8
Developer web site: http://www.algebratouch.com/
Internet required: No

What Is Algebra Touch?

Algebra Touch is for new algebra students, as well as those who want a refresher or to learn new techniques and skills. The app has an explanation and practice area and allows users to create their own problems or even edit current ones. Materials covered include simplification, like terms, commutativity, order of operations, factorization, prime numbers elimination, isolation, variables, basic equations, distribution, factoring out, and more advanced modes.

The practice section, denoted by the bulleted list icon in the iPod Touch version, allows users to practice everything they learned in the teaching section. Each lesson walks the user through the steps and uses the touch screen to teach the concept of algebra. When users need to combine terms, they simply move numbers in the equation so they're next to each other. Algebra Touch is a great hands-on way to manipulate equations and practice concepts. Students learn to drag and rearrange single-variable polynomials so that like terms are together for easier adding. You definitely don't have to wait for formal algebra to hand this app to students, though. Being able to visually see how algebra works can cause the light-bulb to go off for many students.

How Does Algebra Touch Work?

When this app is opened, the user is presented with a simple addition problem on the screen (see Figure 1).

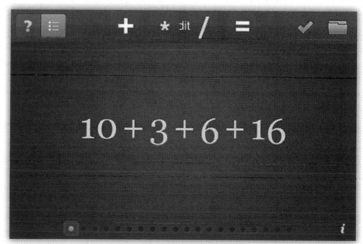

Figure 1—*Opening screen addition*

The app walks the user through math questions with show-me steps (see Figure 2). Algebra Touch will not allow users to do the order of operations incorrectly. When the user taps the wrong operator or attempts to put a number in the wrong place, the problem gives the user a "no-no shake."

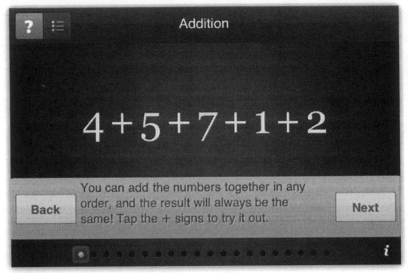

Figure 2—*Show-me steps screen*

To generate a new problem, the iPhone or iPod Touch user will tap on the envelope on the right side of the app; iPad users will click on Generate Problem on the top left side of the screen (see Figure 3).

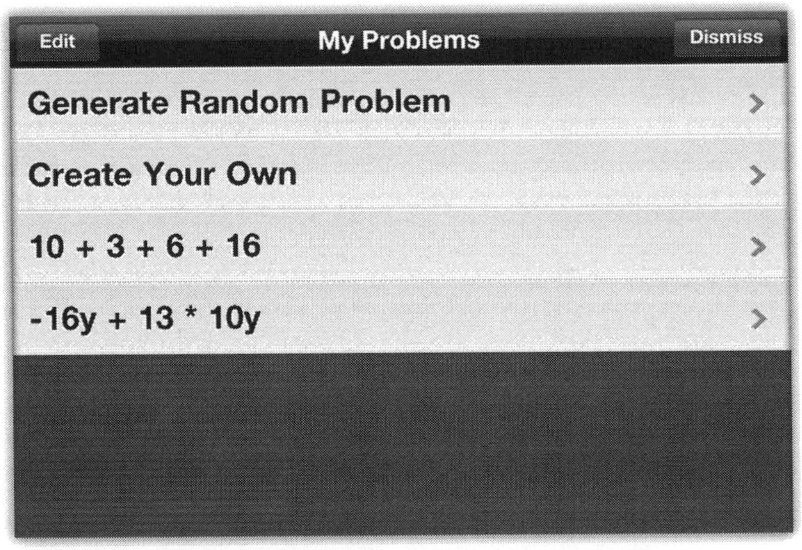

Figure 3—*Generate random problem*

Users can create their own problems by clicking on the pen icon (see Figure 4a) or tapping the operator between the numbers to compute answers (see Figure 4b).

Figure 4a—*Create problem/pen icon*

Figure 4b—*Create problem/tapping operator*

The app can be reset to start the process from simple addition problems to more advanced ones (see Figure 5).

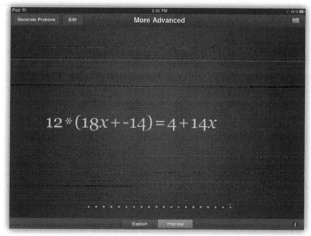

Figure 5—*Advanced problem screen*

Terms can be factored or combined until the variable is isolated. Tapping will compute all the arithmetic automatically except for division, since the app requires fractions to be fully reduced before the answer is correct. Using the app makes understanding the process much easier as we can see in Figures 6a and 6b. The FOIL method happens before us on the screen.

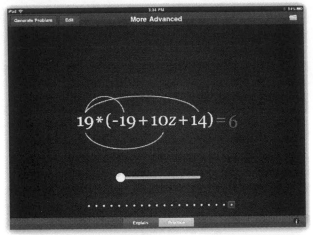

Figure 6a—*Computation process*

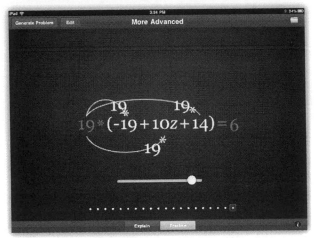

Figure 6b—*FOIL method*

How Can Algebra Touch Be Used in the Classroom?

Algebra Touch allows students to manipulate and solve single-variable algebraic equations and terms in a creative way in the classroom. Students can use this app to learn many basic concepts through clear instruction and practice. The app is great for working commutative property problems. Moving the numbers will let students touch and see that the operation can happen with the numbers in any order. This makes the order of operations make sense. Factorization skills also are exercised with this app, as seen on the following page in Figures 7a and 7b.

Algebra Touch allows for repeated practice of problems generated by the app or created by the user. Repetitive practice of the same problem allows students to talk their way through the steps of answering more difficult questions. The app saves the user-created problems.

With the iPad 2 connected to a projector, Algebra Touch can be used for whole-group instruction. A student could lead a small group because the app will not allow for incorrect answers.

Figure 7a—*Factorization 1*

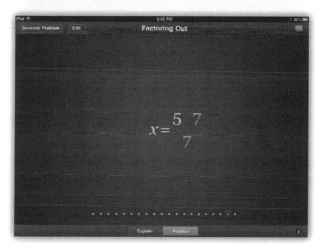

Figure 7b—*Factorization 2*

Screenshots can be taken of the steps of more difficult questions and opened in an annotation app on the iPad. Students can write down what is happening in that part of the question.

The Algebra Touch app is a much better practice tool than a worksheet. The worksheet cannot guide a struggling student to a correct answer. Finally, even if users haven't studied formal algebra before, playing with this app will teach them many basic concepts, especially if they work through the tutorial.

Comic Touch/
Comic Touch Lite

about the app

App name: Comic Touch / Comic Touch Lite
Subject areas: All
Available for: iPad / iPod Touch / iPhone
Cost: $2.99 for iPad / Free for iPhone and iPod Touch
Requirements: Requires iOS 2.2.1 or later.
iTunes URL: http://itunes.apple.com/us/app/comic-touch/id284959707?mt=8
Developer web site: http://plasq.com/products/comictouch/
Internet required: No

What Is Comic Touch?

Comic Touch is an app for creating single-page comics for learning. The essential components of Comic Touch are art and narrative, and they are two things humans have been using to communicate their understanding for generations.

Figure 1—Photo options

The app might seem like a simple idea, but it is a powerful tool with regard to learning. With this app, students can create a visual graphic that contains key information using speech bubbles and caption boxes to describe an image.

How Does Comic Touch Work?

There are several photo editing apps for the iPhone, but Comic Touch is in a class all its own. By allowing you to add text bubbles and hilarious distortions, the possibilities with this app are endless. As you can see in Figure 1, you choose a photo that you would like to use. Once you get your picture the way you want it, adding text is simple.

Tap the text bubble you want and then tap where you want it in the picture, as shown in Figure 2. You can easily move it by tapping and dragging. If you want to delete a bubble, tap and hold it; when the x shows on the left of the bubble, you can tap on the x to delete. You can even move and adjust the stem of the bubble to point it to the place you want it. To add text, double tap on the speech bubble, add your text as seen in Figure 3, and then click Done.

Figure 2—*Speech bubble on an image*

Figure 3—*Bubble text entry*

The next window (Figure 4) will allow you to adjust the details of the text, as well as the font size and the color scheme of the bubble. Once you have the text you want, you can play around with the distortions as in Figure 5. To do this, tap the second to the left button on the top toolbar and then tap where you want the distortion to be centered.

Figure 4—*Font and color choices*

Figure 5—*Distortion effects*

These distortions can be removed by clicking on None. Keeping the photo "Full size" and the option to save it to the photo library are shown in Figure 6. The next option allows you save the comic to photos or email it to someone (Figure 7).

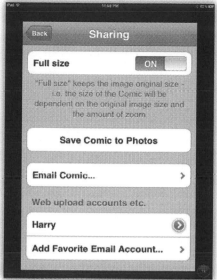

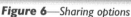

Figure 6—*Sharing options*   *Figure 7*—*Email comic*

Figure 8 shows a feature that allows the user to create a favorite email address to send the comics to. This allows for the process of sending comics to be more efficient. This could be a teacher's email address or the address to a blog on the subject the class is covering. Comics you have created can be seen as a group when you click on the fourth icon. The last option on the top of the page is deleting; just tap on the trashcan, and any changes made to an image are deleted. Comic Touch brings photos to life with balloons that give the subject words and thoughts (Figure 9).

Figure 8—*Editing email options*   *Figure 9*—*Using other balloon styles*

How Can Comic Touch Be Used in the Classroom?

Comics are really a way of outlining things that you know. Events can be put into a sequence, and you can choose what characters say as well as what an event or graphic may mean. Visual images can be used to convey meaning, and creating comics helps students develop creativity and higher-level thought processing. Comics can be used to re-create a moment in history, and with pictures from the photo library, steps in a process can be traced with images. Using Comic Touch, students can create an analysis of events, debate the pros and cons of products, express their position on a historical event, and more.

Using Comic Touch, students can tell their story that no one would hear otherwise, or they can retell an event from their own perspective.

Figure 10—*I Have a Dream*

The app allows the user to save an image as a photo or email it to classmates or teachers. Comic Touch can be used in every classroom to allow students to present what they know in a digital format. The app also could be used to examine social, political, and economic changes by adding speech bubbles to images.

As you can see in Figure 10, with this image of Dr. Martin Luther King Jr., students can re-create moments in history. Using Comic Touch, teachers and students can show the correct way of solving a problem and the correct steps needed to reach a solution. Key concepts are easier to remember when a graphic contains important information.

In Figure 11, you can see how an acute angle is illustrated and labeled. Comic Touch can be used to model and identify circle, radius, diameter, center, and circumference. Students could model and identify the properties of congruent figures with captions and speech bubbles. When reading scientific and technical texts, students need to be able to gain knowledge from challenging texts that often make extensive

Figure 11—*A new twist on acute angles*

use of elaborate diagrams and data to convey information and illustrate concepts. In a science classroom, students could give a voice to objects they are studying in science, such as different types of leaves, the planets, human anatomy, and more. In a fine arts class, scenes from a Shakespeare play can be reproduced from images of students in costume. In an English language arts class, students can re-create dialogue from a video clip or a movie.

Students can use Comic Touch to develop written or visual messages in a foreign language. Comic Touch can be used by students to interact in writing in a foreign language. Students can demonstrate their understanding of the commodities, for example, of the Spanish-speaking world by creating an infomercial using Comic Touch. This could be a cross-curricular activity with an economics class. Students can use Spanish or other foreign languages in the classroom, school, and beyond by creating skits using Comic Touch to put their ideas in digital ink. This would be a great app to use when creating a cross-curricular activity between the foreign language classes and any of the other content areas by creating comic strips to answer questions for math, English, social studies, and so on.

In a cross-curricular activity with math and economics, students can use Comic Touch to insert images and describe the food as well as do a comparison of what that food cost and why it may be more or less expensive in a country that has a language other than English as its primary language.

Comic Touch can be used to give brief presentations using learned vocabulary and grammar. Students can produce level-appropriate visual or multimedia demonstrations (e.g., posters, brochures, slide shows, blogs, podcasts, and now comic strips) using an app like Comic Touch.

Be creative and tell a story about simple machines, insects, or photosynthesis (Figure 12). Challenge the students to come up with a funny comic strip that tells a joke about the subject you are studying, especially if it is a subject that people would not expect to have much humor, like science.

Figure 12—*Fun with neutrons!*

Use a similar technique while using a personification of objects or pictures to tell a story (see Figure 13). Have mathematicians get into a debate about their theories. Above all, use humor and remember that this one can be fun.

Figure 13—*Giving a simple object a voice*

EMD PTE

App name: EMD PTE
Subject areas: Science
Available for: iPad / iPod Touch / iPhone
Cost: Free
Requirements: Requires iOS 3.1 or later.
iTunes URL: http://itunes.apple.com/us/app/emd-pte/id377393859?mt=8
Developer web site: http://www.emdchemicals.com/
Internet required: No

What Is EMD PTE?

EMD's interactive "Periodic Table of the Elements for iPhone" app puts a wealth of information on the chemical elements right into your pocket, presented in a user-friendly interface. This app is VGA capable and can be used with a projector. There is an interactive web version of this app on the developer web site.

How Does EMD PTE Work?

When you open EMD PTE, you will see the 112 elements listed on the periodic table (Figure 1). The elements are color coded by classification; nonmetals are red, inert gasses are pink, and so on.

Figure 1—*Periodic table screen*

Interactivity happens with a tap on any element, as you can see in Figure 2 with iodine. The designation, classification, group, period, and relative atomic mass are visible on the first click.

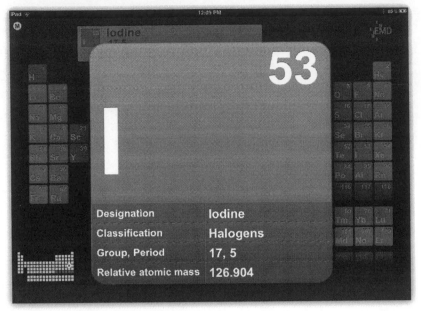

Figure 2—*Examining an element*

If you tap the element again, the icon flips over for you to view other information about the element (Figure 3). It shows basic information along with who discovered the element and a picture of it. Tapping on the screen brings the entire table back into view.

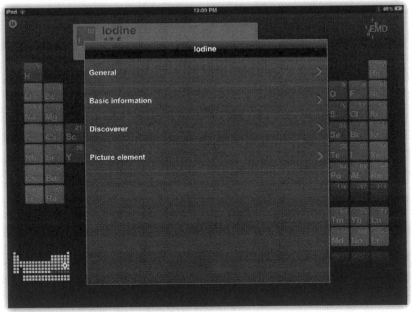

Figure 3—*More element information*

In Figure 4, you see even more options! First is a search window that allows you to search by chemical name. The classifications tab allows users to sort by properties, classifications, and the element's percentage of the Earth's core.

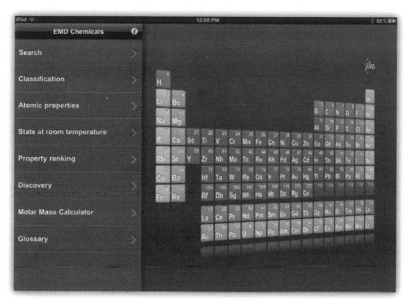

Figure 4—*More table options*

Atomic properties become a visual when the tab is clicked. Elements can be ranked in ascending or descending order by relative atomic mass, melting point, and more. The element's state at room temperature can also be viewed. With his or her finger a user can quickly scroll up or down the scale to see the state of a chemical from -460°F to 10000°F.

How Can EMD PTE Be Used in the Classroom?

Periodic tables need to be interactive, and in classrooms, the period table on the wall doesn't do much when you "click" on it. With EMD PTE, students can find out quickly where the name "lithium" comes from or who discovered molybdenum with two taps on the screen of the iPad. Students and teachers can find the half-life of darmstadtium-281 by clicking on the element's general properties. The PTE app allows you to explore the world of the chemical elements right from your iPad, iPod Touch, or iPhone interactively and intuitively. This outstanding app can be used by students and teachers, or by anyone who wants to learn more about the chemical elements.

In the chemistry classroom, students are required to learn the significance of the periodic table and its historical development. Students can quickly see each element's year of discovery, the country where it was discovered, and who discovered it (refer back to Figure 4). Students and teachers can use this app to quickly see the arrangement of the periodic table based on electron filling orders.

When the elements are grouped, they are highlighted on the screen so they are easier to find. The atomic properties or periodic trends, atomic radius, atomic radius chart, electronegativity, and relative atomic mass become visual with this app. The glossary explains the element's classification, and clicking on the classification then gives the user a visual.

Advanced Uses

The EMD PTE app allows users to scroll up and down the chart to view images of the discoverer and see the history of the element by year from 5000 BC to 2000 AD. This tool could allow science to be infused into a history project from a particular period in time. The EMD PTE app has a molar mass calculator to calculate chemical formulas. Students can also use the ionization energy chart to assist them with the prediction of bonding type of compounds.

Frog Dissection

about the app

App name: Frog Dissection
Subject areas: Science
Available for: iPad 1 and 2
Cost: $3.99
Requirements: Requires iOS 4.1 or later.
iTunes URL: http://itunes.apple.com/us/app/frog-dissection/id377626675?mt=8
Developer web site: http://www.punflay.com/virtual-frog.html
Internet required: Yes, to link to the videos and other online video resources

What Is Frog Dissection?

Frog Dissection, a simulation of a frog dissection and reference materials about frogs, is a middle and high school science and biology application. The full video mirroring in the iPad 2 will allow this application to be easily shared via a projector or monitor.

How Does Frog Dissection Work?

Frog Dissection is a biological simulation and information resource. Using the simulation, students are able to dissect a frog and compare human and frog biology. A simple testing system allows users to quiz themselves and provides simple feedback on depth of understanding. The virtual nature of the tool allows the dissection to be rehearsed and replayed as often as is required.

How Can Frog Dissection Be Used in the Classroom?

This application has eight component sections:

- Frog dissection—simulation
- All about frog
- Humans vs. frogs
- Wet lab process
- Quiz
- Internal organs 3D
- Videos
- Types of frogs

The key component is a simulation of a dissection of a frog. With clear spoken instructions and accurate simulations, the dissection takes the learners step-by-step through an abdominal and thoracic dissection of the frog. Students are presented with a selection of tools and are required to follow the steps to complete the dissection. Once the dissection is complete, learners can click on the various organs to load new pages with descriptive materials on the purpose and function of the organ. The animations are crisp and clean.

The second component of the application is the "All About Frog" element, shown in Figures 1a and 1b. This is a reference section, which covers most aspects of the key information regarding frogs. It covers the following:

- Classification

- Eating and living

- Appearance

- Special senses

- Life cycle

- Digestive system

- Organs

- Ecosystem

- Frogs and toads comparison.

The frogs versus humans section compares the amphibian to mammals, using the frog and human as examples of each vertebrate class. This section examines the cardiovascular, respiratory, and digestive systems and also provides a general overview. The series of instructional slides on wet lab procedures for the frog dissection provides more than 19 slides to guide learners through the process (see Figures 2 and 3).

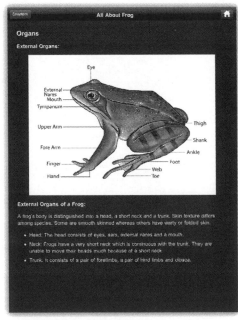

Figure 1a—*All About Frog*

Figure 1b—*Types of Frogs*

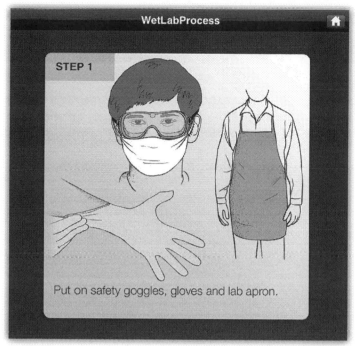

Figure 2—*Wet lab prep sample frame*

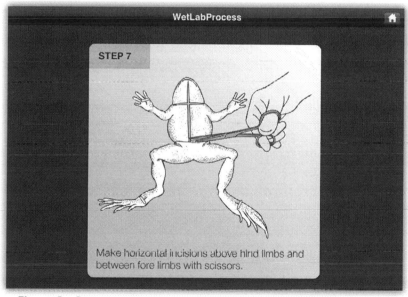

Figure 3—*Dissection instruction sample*

Each slide has a clear instruction that mirrors the process of a live dissection through a simulation instead. The quiz tool provides a simple testing tool with randomly selected questions. The questions are available in multiple-choice format with the question and answer being read out aloud to the learners. Audio and visual cues inform students of the accuracy of their answers.

The 3D internal organs provide written and audio commentary about the role and function of various internal organs. The video section, while limited at the time of writing, looks at some of the behavioral aspects of the frog.

Classroom Application

Frog Dissection is applicable across the middle and high school as a reference resource for amphibians and specifically frogs. The frog versus human section allows simple comparative biology between mammals and amphibians. The other reference material provides a useful resource for student projects on amphibians. Students are provided simple stimulus material on the habitat and niche that the frog occupies.

For senior students, the simulation provides excellent reinforcement or rehearsal for an actual frog dissection but can also serve as an alternative to dissecting frogs. Additionally, the ability to repeat and review the dissection at the learner's leisure is a powerful aid to learning. The reference material provides a good entry point for research into frogs and a good starting point for examining and discussing comparative anatomy. The comparison examines the respiratory system, circulatory systems, digestive tract and organs, and a general comparison of mammals and amphibians. The material lacks the depth needed to be a complete reference but does provide pleasing starting points. The key feature for the application is, however, the dissection.

Related Applications: Rat Dissection

Rat Dissection is a separate purchase from the virtual frog dissection. While not too well developed yet, Rat Dissection fills a similar niche to Frog Dissection. In a series of 11 steps, students can dissect the abdominal and thoracic cavities of the rat, and then examine the internal organs individually. As in Frog Dissection, the audio commentary is useful and informative.

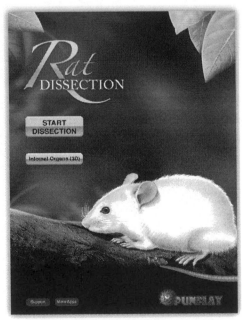

Figure 4—*Rat Dissection: Home screen*

gFlashPro

App name: gFlashPro Flashcards and Test
Subject areas: All
Available for: iPad / iPod Touch / iPhone
Cost: $3.99
Requirements: Requires iOS 3.2 or later.
iTunes URL: http://itunes.apple.com/us/app/gflashpro-flashcards-tests/id297332787?mt=8
Developer web site: http://www.gwhizmobile.com/Desktop/gFlash.php
Internet required: Yes, to access flash card sets that have to be downloaded

What Is gFlashPro?

With the gFlashPro Flashcards and Test app, students and teachers can create and edit cards on the iPad or in Google Docs and access card sets from StudyStack™, FlashcardExchange, WinFlash Educator, gWhiz, and Quizlet.

How Does gFlashPro Work?

An Internet connection is needed to download flashcard sets. A Google account is needed to create flashcards with Google Spreadsheets. There are additional charges for flashcard sets from some of the creators. In Figure 1, users can choose from StudyStack, gWhiz Catalog, and Quizlet or create their own flashcards through the gFlashPro Editor or Google Docs. To download, select the desired source—once the flashcard set is downloaded, the cards are put in the downloaded group on the home screen.

Figure 1—Adding card sets

To open a downloaded set of cards, tap on the flashcard set. In Figures 2 and 3, the peroidic table of elements is chosen. The atomic symbol is on one side of the card and the element names to choose from are on the other.

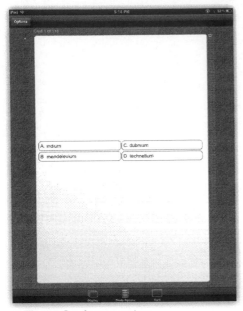

Figure 2—*Answer options*

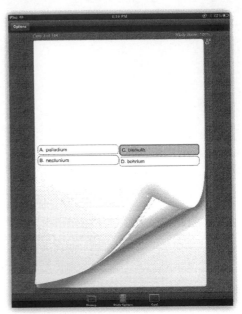

Figure 3—*Choosing an answer*

When the correct answer is chosen, it is highlighted in green. Incorrect answers are highlighted in red and users are given the correct answer on the screen. Cards can be displayed in one- or two-card view (Figure 4). Study options are reverse Q & A and multiple choice. Cards can be reshuffled for new users. Clicking on the information tab, users get instructions on the home screen and the features guide (Figure 5).

Figure 4—*Two-card view*

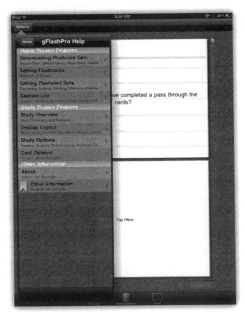

Figure 5—*Help menu options*

Questions Created in Google Spreadsheets

This is a two-column format—column A is question and B is answer. Column B can also be used as a source of three alternative answers when viewed in multiple-choice mode. The app supports hosted image URLs for questions and answers in all modes including multiple choice. One question (Column A) with up to five unique answers (Columns B thru F) can also be created using Google Spreadsheets.

How Can gFlashPro Be Used in the Classroom?

There are several applications on the market for mobile learning in the classroom. These will allow you to customize content to your specifications and at low cost. The gFlashPro app by gWhiz Mobile has come up with flashcards and trivia questions on a number of subjects that are downloadable. Users can create cards that exercise and strengthen rote memory through the Google Documents web site to control what students will be practicing through this app. Figures 6a through 6d show some mathematics and science examples.

Figure 6a—Geometry

Figure 6b—Algebra

Figure 6c—Chemistry

Figure 6d—Physics

Flashcard information is also available through StudyStack and Flashcard Exchange that places an extensive list of resources with hundreds of thousands of facts at students' fingertips. When the app is opened, you are given the option to download from any of these three sources and get started immediately. There are thousands of contributed flashcard sets in gWhiz, Quizlet has a 2.5-million+ flashcard set repository, and StudyStack has a great repository of flashcards and study activities.

The gFlash app is one of the fullest functioning flashcard programs the AppStore has to offer. This has the benefit of hitting that target edutainment audience. Students can use the flashcards to study for exams or learn trivia, or for personal enrichment. This isn't a necessarily boring or pedantic (if you don't know what this mean, maybe a vocabulary flashcard set is in order) endeavor. There is some truly enlightening information out there that you can find with this app.

The interface is really easy to use. It switches between portrait and landscape mode smoothly based on your use of the accelerometer. You can change from a one-card view to a two-card view where you tap the second card to reveal your answer. You can play it Jeopardy style and guess the question for the answer. There is the option either to keep track of your score or to play scoreless. Also, you are not limited to just text. The app also includes videos, sounds, and images that do much to enhance the whole experience.

Using Google Spreadsheets, teachers can create and share flashcard sets with students or other teachers, and students can create their own study guides. gWhiz has created several K–12 flashcard sets with Florida Virtual Schools, McGraw-Hill, and others—these can be found on the gWhiz web site (http://www.gwhizmobile.com/Desktop/Products. php). Students and teachers can combine or copy card sets. This is especially helpful when the number of cards continues to increase. Users can also navigate through card sets with a swipe of the finger and permanently delete a card in the gFlashPro editor. Also available from gWhiz are templates for creating two-column, multiple-choice test question multisided flashcards, flashcards with video files, and more. The templates are available at http://www.gwhizmobile.com/Desktop/creating.php.

iMathematics

App name: iMathematics
Subject areas: Mathematics
Available for: iPad 1 and 2 / iPod Touch / iPhone
Cost: Free version with option for in-app purchase
Requirements: Requires iOS 3.2 or later.
iTunes URL: http://itunes.apple.com/uy/app/imathematics-9-in-1/id337535181?mt=8
Developer web site: http://smokinapps.com/developer/antonio-giarrusso/
Internet required: Only to connect to external links

What Is iMathematics?

The iMathematics app is a high school mathematical resource with calculators and equation solving tools. Resource and reference materials are included for most disciplines within the mathematics curriculum. Much of the content is available in the free edition, but full content is unlocked in the pro version.

How Does iMathematics Work?

This application provides definitions and examples of key mathematical concepts with examples to illustrate each concept. Each page has links to web-based resources to provide extensions and further information.

There are more than 700 concepts and formulas explored in the product. The free content includes material for the following areas:

- Arithmetic
- Algebra
- Plane geometry
- Solid geometry
- Analytic geometry
- Goniometry
- Analysis
- Trigonometry

The iMathematics app's forms provide a range of resources for reference in mathematics. Some references are only available in the pro version (see Figure 1).

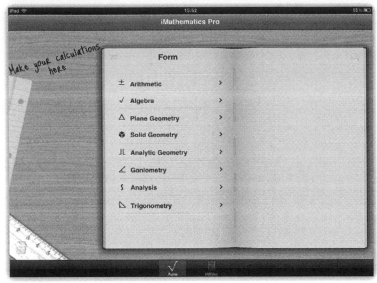

Figure 1—*iMathematics forms*

Features

The utilities section contains a number of useful tools, including these:

- Basic and advanced calculator (the graphical calculator is a pro version unlock)

- Equation solver

- Fraction approximator

- Matrix and system solver (pro version)

- Quick form—24-page glossary (pro version)

A number of other features are available in the pro edition. The forms and utilities sections both have areas to write notes or calculations (Figure 2), but unfortunately these are not saved or recordable. The advanced calculator uses the wolfgram-alpha computational search engine and as such requires Internet connectivity. In the pro version, there are approximately 50 quizzes or short tests associated with the different topics. This is a useful feature for informing learning as it allows students to self-direct their learning.

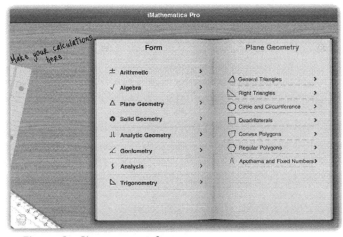

Figure 2—*Plane geometry form*

The "tips and tricks" section provides an extension and enrichment element as it provides interesting historical and process snippets for the passionate and curious student.

How Can iMathematics Be Used in the Classroom?

The iMathematics app is a useful tool within and outside of the classroom environment. Used as a reference, it exceeds the requirements of most mathematical courses at the high school level. However, the utilities allow students to have a more holistic approach to study and learning.

Students are encouraged to use the calculation/workspace area to solve a problem and then select the appropriate solution tool to calculate the correct answer. Students can swap between the forms (reference material) and utilities without losing material written in the workspace. Being able to easily move between research (forms), application of research (workspace), and using the solution tools in the utilities makes for a beneficial learning environment. The utilties menu has a variety of different tools including graphic calculators, as shown in Figure 3.

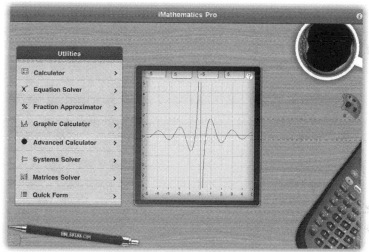

Figure 3—*Graphic calculator*

Students reading and working through the different reference elements can test their understanding of the concepts and theory by taking the flash tests. This provides instant feedback and highlights the areas of weakness and strength.

The tips and tricks provide extensions and background for the curious student. The links to external web sites, such as Wikipedia, provide an avenue for further development of the knowledge and skills base or a different explanation.

The nature of mathematics at the high school level does require a basis of knowledge for students to be able to use the tools, resources, and materials in this application effectively. This application is not a mathematics textbook providing exercises for skill development and reinforcement; rather, it is a reference tool for the underlying concepts.

Manual for the
United States
of America

App name: Manual for the United States of America

Subject areas: Social studies, U.S. history

Available for: iPad / iPod Touch / iPhone

Cost: $2.99

Requirements: Requires iOS 3.2 or later.

iTunes URL: http://itunes.apple.com/us/app/manual-for-united-states-america/id290560026?mt=8

Developer web site: http://cbagwellconsulting.com/

Internet required: Yes, to download additional writings and latest developments in U.S. officials

What Is Manual for the United States of America?

Manual for the United States of America gives students the opportunity to investigate the historical foundations of the United States government.

How Does Manual for the United States of America Work?

When the app is opened (Figure 1), users can choose to download additional content or choose to use content including the Declaration of Independence, the Constitution, information on the states, the latest developments in government, and more.

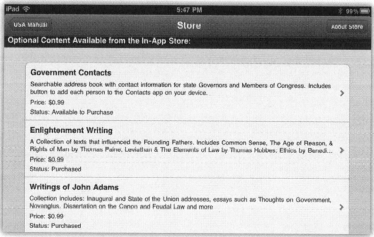

Figure 1—Store menu

How Can Manual for the United States of America Be Used in the Classroom?

The Manual for the United States of America app can be easily incorporated into a civics or American government class. From the Declaration of Independence to current change in the elected officials in Washington, D.C., this app is the answer. In the Declaration of Independence area of the app, students and teachers will find the main text, the signers, and short biographies of the signers (Figure 2).

In the Constitution area of the app, students can investigate the major governmental ideas. Students can use the app to quickly find the Articles of the United States Constitution and notes attached to them. The Preamble, and notes about the Preamble, are in the app. The signers and their biographies, along with original images of the document, are also included.

Other documents included are the Articles of Confederation, George Washington's farewell address, the Civil Rights Act of 1964, and others. There are historical documents that led to the development of the United States Constitution. There is also a document that explains how laws are made, which was created by Charles W. Johnson, a parliamentarian for the U.S. House of Representatives.

Figure 2—*Biography sample page*

Figure 3—*Supreme Court cases*

Supreme Court cases with landmark opinions are in the app also (Figure 3). Other in-app purchases can be made to enhance the app more. These include the writings of John Adams, Thomas Jefferson, and other writers who influenced the Founding Fathers. In addition, you can find *The Elements of Law* by Thomas Hobbes, *The Age of Reason* by Thomas Paine, and *Two Treatises of Government* by John Locke. Presidential facts and Supreme Court justice facts can be viewed in the app as well.

For a civics class, much of the information needed is included inside the app. In an American government class, students can analyze the purpose of government through the readings and gain knowledge to explain the importance of the historical documents, events, and people that led to the development of the United States Constitution (see Figures 4 and 5). U.S. State senators and representatives are listed and updated.

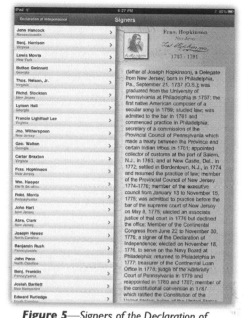

Figure 4—*Signers of the Constitution*

Figure 5—*Signers of the Declaration of Independence*

A link to a state map with direction options and the state's web site are available in the app for each state. Hard copy textbooks cannot offer up-to-date features. The Manual for the United States of America also includes some quick facts about each state, including capital names and information on leading government officials.

NASA App HD

about the app

App name: NASA App HD
Subject areas: Science, social studies, geography
Available for: iPad 1 and 2 / iPod Touch / iPhone
Cost: Free
Requirements: Requires iOS 3.2 or later.
iTunes URL: http://itunes.apple.com/ca/app/nasa-app-hd/id387310098?mt=8
Developer web site: http://www.nasa.gov/centers/ames/iphone/index.html
Internet required: Yes

What Is NASA App HD?

NASA App HD is a free science and humanities app developed by NASA and available in both HD format for the iPad and standard format for the iPhone and iPod Touch. The application is a reference and news tool, allowing students to see featured blogs, updates, and the current launch schedule for missions, as well as to explore the reference material available. The application supports streamed videos from NASA on a variety of topics and areas of interest.

Figure 1—*NASA App HD splash screen*

Figure 2—*Upper toolbar options*

How Does NASA App HD Work?

The toolbar on the top (see Figure 2) links to a variety of different features and tools. These include the following:

- *Featured content*—This is a great reference tool, alphabetically listing key content. The content contains links to images and updates, including the ISS (international space station) tracker.

- *Calendar*—This is a launch and mission calendar for NASA missions and provides a calendar up to a year in advance detailing launch vehicles, objectives, and so on.

- *NASA centers*—This is a Google map link that shows the NASA facilities and centers. Clicking on marker pins brings up specific information about the center and links to the center's web site.

- *News feed*—This provides news topics and features about NASA. The feed is broken into different components, such as the shuttle, Mars and the moon, solar systems, the universe, the Earth, aeronautics, technology, and NASA jobs and people. The feeds are arranged by age, showing you the newest material first. Feeds can be linked to Twitter, email, or Facebook.

- *Solar system*—This is the opening or default view for the application. It displays the sun and the planets as they are arranged around the sun. Clicking on a celestial object will bring up a detailed information page (or pages) about the body in question.

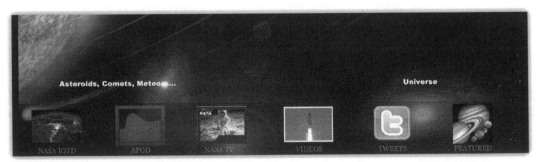

Figure 3—*Lower toolbar options*

The lower toolbar (see Figure 3) allows students to access a powerful array of resources ranging from featured content to video clips and NASA TV as well as the regularly updated featured link. The lower toolbar has both the NASA IOTD (image of the day) and APOD (astronomy picture of the day) links. These are amazing images from NASA or a number of other sources.

How Can NASA App HD Be Used in the Classroom?

The NASA application provides a powerful reference tool not only for space-focused lessons and units but also to explore the range of areas of interest and exploration that NASA is involved in. This tool fits smartly into both the social studies and science curricula.

In the science curriculum, as students learn about our planet and beyond, they can explore the different planets and regions of our solar system by quickly accessing a valid and reliable resource. Using the image galleries, APOD, and IOTD, they can access high-quality imagery, supported by detailed captions explaining the significance and history of each image. The video archive can be accessed using either a simple keyword search or the more powerful advanced search. These videos provide students with access to resources that would not normally be available in the classroom. A search for Apollo will reveal more than 75 video clips ranging from mission footage to reflections by the astronauts (see Figure 4).

Figure 4—*Video archive results for "Apollo"*

In the social studies classroom, the NASA app provides resource material and insight into the challenges, frustrations, and successes of the space race. The historical images and commentaries provide a unique perspective as students delve into the final frontier of exploration—space.

Closer to home, the Earth section within the news feed provides up-to-date information about current research projects exploring our planet (see Figure 5).

Figure 5—*Earth news feed*

The image archive allows social studies students access to powerful and detailed satellite imagery. These pictures provide a unique insight from a truly amazing perspective on our planet. Carefully constructed searches will allow students to find images and detailed commentary (see Figure 6).

Figure 6—*View of Africa from orbit*

Students can use the NASA application to construct the basic knowledge that will lead to probing and challenging classroom questions, projects, and tasks. Its range of materials and easy format make it a useful and suitable tool for the classroom and a great starting point for higher-order thinking, analysis, and evaluation.

Play2Learn

App name: Play2Learn
Subject areas: Language arts
Available for: iPad / iPod Touch; some applications are available for iPad / iPhone, others are only available in one or the other format.
Cost: $1.99
Requirements: Requires iOS 3.2 or higher.
iTunes URL: http://itunes.apple.com/us/app/play2learn-english-hd/id378746394?mt=8
Developer web site: http://www.play2learn.pl/
Internet required: No

What Is Play2Learn?

Play2Learn is an oral language vocabulary learning and reinforcement tool for a variety of languages including these:

- French
- German
- Chinese
- Italian
- Spanish
- Portuguese
- English
- Polish
- Russian

It also includes a multilingual clock (iPad only).

How Does Play2Learn Work?

Each Play2learn application is purchased individually with extension packs available for a small cost. The application works in two modes:

- *Point and listen*—This is the learning aspect of the application. Learners click on the object and listen to a native language speaker pronounce the term.

- *Listen and point*—This is the testing phase of the application. Learners listen to the term and then touch the appropriate object or part.

Students are rewarded with either applause, or the sound of breaking glass. The successfully answered objects change from transparent to full color (see Figure 1).

Figure 1—*Point and Listen mode*

Figure 2—*Palette selection*

Students select the vocabulary to be learned from a range of palettes (see Figure 2). The palettes are arranged into thematic sets. For example, the Play2Learn French application includes these palette themes:

- Colors
- Shapes
- Family
- Vehicles
- Body parts
- Jewelry
- House

- Fruit and vegetables

- Animals and pets

The hint feature is useful, showing the objects that are active in each page.

How Can Play2Learn Be Used in the Classroom?

Learning languages requires mastery of not only the written aspects of the language but also the spoken or oral aspects. Recognizing the spoken elements of the language is critical. The use of native language speakers is powerful as the pronunciation of the words and the emphasis on the different syllables are critical to correct speech.

Learners are provided with the opportunity to listen to the spoken word as frequently as is required to learn the term, as they work through each thematic palette. They can also repeat the process as often as necessary. Once learners have a degree of confidence, the process is reversed. Students listen to the spoken word and touch the appropriate element. Instant feedback in the form of applause or breaking glass provides immediate reinforcement of success.

This is an activity that can be done individually, in small groups, or with suitable hardware connected to a projector or interactive whiteboard. The use of related themes makes learning specific language sets and rehearsing pronunciation easy.

This is a tool that is applicable across all learning levels. It is captivating for younger students, while still being fun for the older learner.

Rory's Story Cubes

App name: Rory's Story Cubes
Subject areas: English language arts, drama
Available for: iPad / iPod Touch / iPhone
Cost: $1.99
Requirements: Requires iOS 3.1.2 or later.
iTunes URL: http://itunes.apple.com/us/app/rorys-story-cubes/id342808551?mt=8
Developer web site: http://www.storycubes.com/products/iphone/
Internet required: No

about the app

What Is Rory's Story Cubes?

Rory's Story Cubes is a storytelling generator that uses nine cubes to give more than 10 million combinations for the foundation of a story. Begin with "Once upon a time," and tell

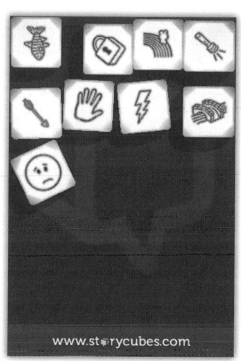

Figure I—*Opening screen*

a story that links together all nine face-up images. Arrange the cubes in any order to start and finish a story. Rory's Story Cubes can be enjoyed by a single student, by taking turns with multiple players, or in groups. There is no wrong answer—the goal is to let the cubes spark students' imagination. Rory's Story Cubes helps students with expository, narrative, descriptive, and persuasive writing.

How Does Rory's Story Cubes Work?

When they open the app, users will see the nine cubes on the screen (Figure 1). There are five icons at the bottom of the page; the first icon shakes the cubes without users having to shake the iPad (this is good for the iPad). A camera icon is for taking a picture of the screen; the picture is saved to the photo library and can be emailed to students.

The next icon (Figure 2) is "how to play" and other information about the app. The next icon turns the sound on and off, and the last icon locks the cubes into place. With a finger, the cubes can be moved around the screen and placed in any order. If a cube is upside down, just tap on the cube and it will turn. This is an app that was created for the iPhone or iPod Touch—on the iPad, click on the 2x in the right corner to double the size for the iPad (Figure 3).

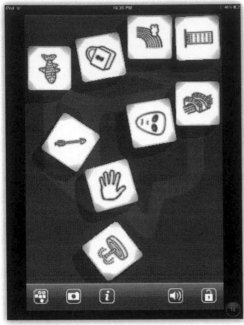

Figure 2—Story Cube options icons

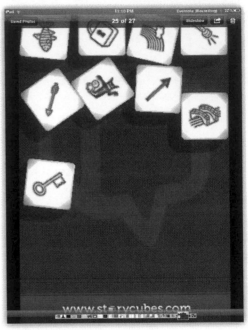

Figure 3—View for the iPad

How Can Rory's Story Cubes Be Used in the Classroom?

Rory's Story Cubes is great for writing stories. The creators of the story cubes recommend that you begin with "Once upon a time…" but you could just as easily start with "It was a dark and stormy night," or "In a land far, far away…" or any other phrase you invent. As their web site says, the cubes are "an infinite story generator." Rory's Story Cubes is an invitation to shared creative thinking, just open-ended enough to encourage spontaneity and humor, just structured enough to maintain focus and challenge.

Have students pick a cube to help them demonstrate effective oral communication. For example, one cube face is a cell phone. This would be a great way to discuss if cell phones could be a useful addition to classroom instruction. Students in a creative writing class could pick one or more cubes to start a discussion about their future plans. One cube face has a picture of a footprint. What a great way to start a story with "Once upon a time." Students often have a blank stare when it is time to write. The cubes give them a visual writing prompt and essay tool to get them started. Students can pick a cube and use precise vocabulary to name and describe known items. Encourage the use of synonyms when describing the action and the objective presented in a story. Using antonyms to describe objects always makes a storytelling activity more exciting. One great activity for students is to take a snapshot of the nine cubes. Give several groups or individual students the same snapshot and allow them to write a story based on the nine cubes.

Another activity is to use the cubes as clues to solve a mystery. Using descriptive words is a must in this exercise. The cubes can also be used as story starters when writing for school, or when stuck on a fiction story. Roll the cubes, have one person arrange them, and the other person has to tell the story. Then switch. Line up all nine cubes in a random order and tell a story in that order, perhaps in a limited amount of time. Roll the cubes and write down as many synonyms or other words for the image on the cube as possible. Before rolling the cubes, pick a topic for the group. Then each person rolls the cubes and tells a story about that topic, working the images into the story. Use each image on the cubes and create a drawing or wordless book that includes them all.

You can also use the cubes in improv acting, having each of the players take a cube or two to work into the scene. If you want a competitive game, have each person roll all nine cubes, and time their story to see who has the shortest story that still makes sense. Use either set when trying to learn a foreign language, to help learn new vocabulary words. The actions cubes really help with practicing verb tenses.

An apptivity for students could be Story Cubes and Dragon Dictation. The student can roll the cubes and create a short story using the audio-to-text features of the Dragon Dictation app (see Figures 4a and 4b). This could be a way of creating observation in a science class or reciting the steps to a complex math problem. It could also be a way for students to show teachers how they are solving problems that may have several steps. If there is a problem in the process the text should show it.

www.storycubes.com

Figure 4a—*Roll the dice...*

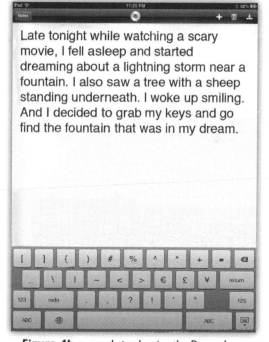

Late tonight while watching a scary movie, I fell asleep and started dreaming about a lightning storm near a fountain. I also saw a tree with a sheep standing underneath. I woke up smiling. And I decided to grab my keys and go find the fountain that was in my dream.

Figure 4b— *...and speak using the Dragon!*

Story Cubes could be used with Whiteboard HD to create a Storyboard from captured images. Story Cubes could also be used with Comic Touch or Strip Designer to create a comic strip from the Story Cube roll.

Shmoop

about the app

App name: Shmoop
Subject areas: English language arts, U.S. history, civics, social studies
Available for: iPad / iPod Touch / iPhone
Cost: $1.99
Requirements: Requires iOS 3.0 or later.
iTunes URL: http://itunes.apple.com/us/app/to-kill-mockingbird-study/id327434694?mt=8
Developer web site: http://www.shmoop.com/
Internet required: Yes, for weblinks

What Is Shmoop?

Shmoop offers academically rigorous learning guides in seven subjects: literature, poetry, best sellers, U.S. history, civics, biography, and music. Written by experts and educators, Shmoop Learning Guides contain deep analysis, questions, quotes, and multimedia. Shmoop uses a conversational tone in combination with pop culture, trivia, and humor to help make topics approachable and relevant to high school students.

How Does Shmoop Work?

Shmoop has several categories to choose from when using a guide, such as the one for *To Kill a Mockingbird*. The study guide's first category is "In a Nutshell" (Figure 1). In a Nutshell gives users a historical background of the work.

Another category users can choose is called "Why Should I Care?" Study guide questions are also another category to choose.

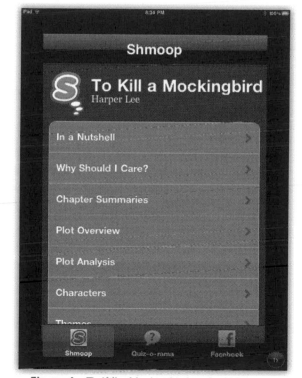

Figure 1—To Kill a Mockingbird *study guide*

In Figure 2, the Quiz-o-Rama is started. There is a Facebook connect where users can challenge friends on Facebook after finishing a quiz (Figure 3).

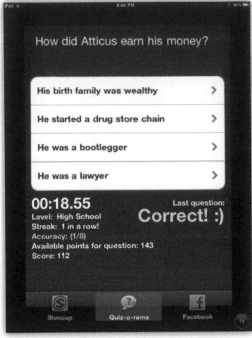

Figure 2—*Taking the quiz*

Figure 3—*Challenging friends*

How Can Shmoop Be Used in the Classroom?

Shmoop helps educators answer this question through its digital resources that make learning fun and relevant for students. The online resource uses relevant and current cultural points of reference to help students see how inspiring and useful these subjects are to their daily lives. A conversational writing tone is also used to make topics both approachable and accessible for students.

How Can the Shmoop App Be Applied to *To Kill a Mockingbird*?

Students apply the knowledge of literary elements to a new literary form, the novel, and discuss the similarities and differences between how those elements are developed in short stories and in novels. Informational texts illuminate the historical context of the Great Depression and the Jim Crow South. In the *To Kill a Mockingbird* study guide, there are chapter summaries, a plot overview, a plot analysis, character information, themes, and quotes.

The following review comes from Teacher Resources in the Media section on the Schmoop web site: "Shmoop's resources help students understand that what they study is applicable to their lives. The app blends intellectual rigor, wit, passion, and pop culture. Rather than hunting the Internet for trustworthy resources, teachers and students can now turn to Shmoop."

Students can use the Shmoop study guides to develop their understanding of the history of novels as a literary form. Recognizing the importance of historical context to the appreciation of setting and character is enhanced with the plot overviews and plot analysis of the app. Students can use the character analysis to identify and analyze major and minor characters.

Students come to understand that novels may have more than one plot, as seen in *To Kill a Mockingbird*. The "Why is it important to me" tab helps students recognize the importance of point of view in *To Kill a Mockingbird* and why it wouldn't be the same story if it had been told from someone else's point of view.

The app can be used to help students determine a theme or central idea of a text and analyze in detail its development over the course of the text, including how it emerges and how it is shaped and refined by specific details. The Themes tab in the Shmoop app for *To Kill a Mockingbird* includes race, justice, judgment, youth, morality, ethics, fear, women, family, and compassion and forgiveness. Using Shmoop, students are assisted in analyzing how complex characters develop over the course of a text, interact with other characters, and advance the plot or develop the theme.

Advanced Uses

Students can present several photographs of small southern towns during the depression from Dorothea Lange's or the Library of Congress's collections and compare them with the description of Maycomb in *To Kill a Mockingbird*. Say which rendering is more vivid to users and explain why.

Other examples from Shmoop are *Anne Frank: Diary of a Young Girl* and Causes of the Civil War (Figures 4 and 5).

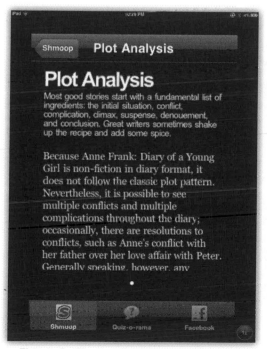

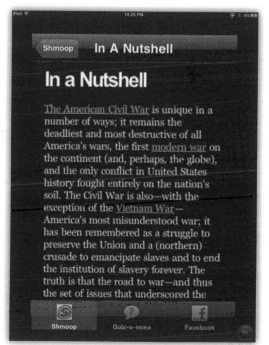

Figure 4—*Plot analysis for* Anne Frank   **Figure 5**—*Civil War "In a Nutshell"*

The Civil War app could be used by students in a world history class as a template or a springboard to discuss civil wars happening around the world today.

Doing this makes the learning real and relevant. Students can ask questions such as "Does a civil war only affect the country having the internal problems? Do other countries involve themselves in the conflict, and why? Did other countries have an interest in the U.S. Civil War?"

Here's another interesting example for using Schmoop in a creative way. When studying the economics of the early 1980s, Shmoop's discussion on Bruce Springsteen's *Born in the U.S.A.* could provide a unique point of view.

Stack the States/ Stack the Countries

App name: Stack the States / Stack the Countries
Subject area: Social sciences, history
Available for: iPad / iPod Touch / iPhone
Cost: $0.99 for iPad / Free for iPhone and iPod Touch
Requirements: Requires iOS 3.0 or later.
iTunes URL: http://itunes.apple.com/us/app/stack-the-states/id381342267?mt=8
Developer web site: http://dan-russell-pinson.com/blog/games.asp
Internet required: Yes

What Is Stack the States?

Stack the States is an educational and fun geography puzzle game. The app asks trivia questions about a state, or asks you to identify the shape of the state (Figure 1).

Figure 1—State trivia questions

If you answer correctly, you'll earn that state to add to your platform. The goal is to stack as many states on the platform as necessary to reach a goal line without the stack tipping over (Figures 2 and 3).

Figure 2—Completing a stack

Figure 3—Stacking platform

The game is fairly simple and is fun to play. Many people have geography skills that need sharpening. In Stack the States, users are asked various questions about the 50 states including capitals, state shapes, abbreviations, bordering states, location on the map, and even nicknames. If you choose the correct state, you get to actually pick it up, move it, rotate it, and place it wherever you want. Your goal is to carefully create a stack of states that reaches the checkered line.

How Does Stack the Countries Work?

Stack the Countries is similar to Stack the States. Users can play on one continent at a time or practice with flashcards when they click on Learn from the main menu.

Figure 4—Stack the Countries

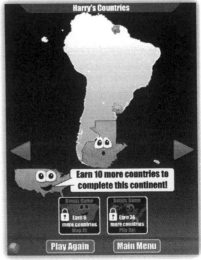

Figure 5—Final score screen

The game focuses on basic country information such as capitals, landmarks, major cities, continents, border countries, languages, flags, and more. You can dive right in and play or brush up on your country knowledge by using the 192 country flashcards and the interactive maps of the continents. As users progress in the game, they earn more countries to add to their personalized map of the world. There are two bonus games that can be unlocked.

How Can Stack the States and Stack the Countries Be Used in the Classroom?

This is a great way to introduce students to other countries in a world history class. They get a visual on how large or small the countries are and what continent they are located on. In the learning part of the game, users can see the major cities of a country, landmarks, and the country's official language. The questions can be limited to as few as two facts up to eight.

The main game isn't timed, so it's a great way for students to learn more about the 50 states, even if they're new to this aspect of geography. Earning all of the states and unlocking the bonus games helps keep things interesting. There is no control over what types of questions are being asked, so this app may not be ideal for a child learning a specific aspect of state trivia (such as the capitals), as it will quiz on all of the areas at once.

Stack the States will help restore and retain all of those childhood geography lessons. Questions asked are state abbreviations, state capital names, state names from a visual location on the map, state nicknames, bordering states, and more.

When you reach the goal, you are awarded a state to add to your collection. As your collection grows, you earn bonus games. There are three bonus games.

- *Pile Up*—The states pile up and students must tap them to get rid of them before the pile gets too high.

- *Puzzler*—Slide the states around and put them together like a jigsaw puzzle.

- *Capital Drop*—Match states with their capitals.

Stack the States is engaging, while still retaining plenty of educational value.

StoryKit

App name: StoryKit
Subject areas: All
Available for: iPad / iPod Touch / iPhone
Cost: Free
Requirements: Compatible with iPhone, iPod Touch, and iPad. Requires iOS 3.0 or later.
iTunes URL: http://itunes.apple.com/us/app/storykit/id329374595?mt=8
Developer web site: http://en.childrenslibrary.org/
Internet required: Internet connectivity is not required for the app to work. Internet is required to share the story online.

What Is StoryKit?

StoryKit is an electronic storybook. After downloading the free StoryKit app, students can create their own versions of classic picture books. The app provides the ability for these budding authors to write text to change the storyline, illustrate the story with their own drawings, images, or photos, and add sound effects to bring the story to life, and they can lay out an entire book with some easy-to-use drag-and-drop features.

How Does StoryKit Work?

Figure 1 shows the first screen—it has an icon for a new book along with a few classic titles.

Clicking on the info button at the upper left of the screen, users find out the where and why of StoryKit. Clicking on the Arrange button allows users to delete unwanted stories and change the order of the books on the screen.

Figure 1—*Opening screen*

To open a book (Figure 2), users tap on the book cover. Options include Read, Edit, and Share. When reading a storybook, swiping to the left changes the pages in the book. Editing (Figure 3) allows for the rearranging of pages as well as the editing of text.

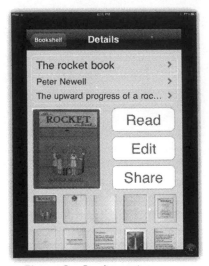

Figure 2—Reading options   *Figure 3*—Edit screen

Creating a New Story With StoryKit

Click on "New Book," and a blank page will appear on the screen. This is the first page of the storybook; images (Figure 4) can be added from the photo library by clicking on the first icon or by clicking on the brush tool, which is the fourth icon on the bottom. Text can be added with the text tool, which is the second icon on the bottom of the screen.

Audio can be added to a story by clicking on the speaker icon, which is the third icon at the bottom of the page. Users can tap the record button to record the audio they want on the page (Figure 5). If you don't like the audio, you can start the recording over simply by clicking the record button again.

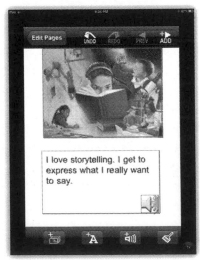

Figure 4—New book   *Figure 5*—Audio recording

To add more pages, click on the Add button in the top right corner of the app. To create the book cover details, click Edit Pages and then Details. The title, the author, and any notes about the story can be added. To share the story online, click on Share, then start sharing (Figure 6). Enter the email address of the person you want to share the story with. It can then be viewed as an online story.

How Can StoryKit Be Used in the Classroom?

StoryKit was designed by researchers at the University of Maryland's Human–Computer Interaction Lab to use in studying how mobile devices could help students enjoy creative and educational activities with members of their families. The idea is that by creating stories on the iPad and iPhone, as opposed to with paper

Figure 6—Sharing options

and pens, children can find time to work on these activities anytime and anywhere.

To teach story writing, StoryKit allows users to place images next to their writing and have it work as a type of book. Students have the ability to present what they know in a digital format. With StoryKit, a student can present text, images, and audio. The creation can be presented by sharing the device, or a link can be sent via email to someone or to a blog for others to see.

StoryKit can be used in the social studies classroom to present the structure and function of government and political institutions. Images for reuse from Flickr and Google or a digital camera could be brought into the story, and students could add audio discussing the parts of government related to the image. A canvas for freehand drawing is part of this app too.

StoryKit can be used in the algebra classroom in solving problems. It can be used by the instructor to explain steps; for example, in Algebra 1, it can be used to demonstrate simplifying radical expressions. Students could also use the app to do the same. Using the iPad and the writing canvas works well. StoryKit can be used in geometry class to identify and describe triangles and their special segments. Measurement problems can be answered with StoryKit using images or photos from Flickr, Google, or an iPad or iPod photo library.

StoryKit can be used in physics to distinguish the difference between nuclear fission and nuclear fusion with images, audio, and text. StoryKit can be a great tool when presenting a science project by communicating your research findings. In English language arts, StoryKit can be used to write elaborate stories with images, audio, and text. Word choice along with vivid descriptions skills can be enhanced with this app.

Students can create simple machine books in science class. They can take pictures from around the school of examples of simple machines with their iPads / iPods and make a digital book using StoryKit, instead of a "hard copy" book.

Students can use DoodleBuddy (free) to add designs to their pictures slides, if they want to draw their own, or they could capture pictures from the Internet.

Other ideas are how-to books for sequencing skills or creating StoryKit stories on Steps of the Scientific Method or Orders of Operations for students who need extra assistance doing this. Students can present their Scientist Study along with their oral presentation. And in a civics class, a student could demonstrate his or her knowledge of state government along with images.

Students can choose myths and legends from a variety of sources: the ancient Greek or Roman civilizations; Russian society; Viking, Eskimo, or Latin American cultures; or other cultures of the students' choice. Or a student could conduct research on a country of choice, and integrate that knowledge with folklore from the same country. Students can use StoryKit to create and write about a real or an imagined experience. Using StoryKit, they could also write and illustrate a story about a country or about the civilizations mentioned above. Since recording is possible, students can also add music in the background to add tone to their stories.

Class discussions could focus on the fact that folklore provides a limited view of a culture and that it's important to research and find out more about the country before making sweeping generalizations about it. Transylvania is often associated with *Dracula* (Bram Stoker's novel and its film adaptations), and the horror genre in general (see Figure 7), while the region is also known for the scenic beauty of its Carpathian landscape and its rich history (see Figure 8). Students could create a short story about the beauty of Transylvania and the people who live there now.

Figure 7—*Bram Stoker's* Dracula

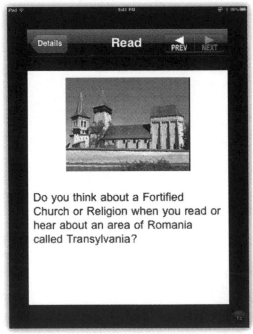

Figure 8—*Transylvania history*

VideoScience

App name: VideoScience
Subject areas: Science
Available for: iPad / iPod Touch / iPhone
Cost: $0.99
Requirements: Requires iOS 4.1 or later.
iTunes URL: http://itunes.apple.com/us/app/videoscience/id333284085?mt=8
Developer web site: http://www.sciencehousefoundation.org/videoscience-experiments.html
Internet required: Yes

What Is VideoScience?

VideoScience is a collection of short videos of science demonstrations designed to serve as a digital colleague and science-teaching companion. With over 80 videos currently, and more added every month, VideoScience helps teachers find inexpensive lab tools and lots of experiments that are easy, effective, and fun for students.

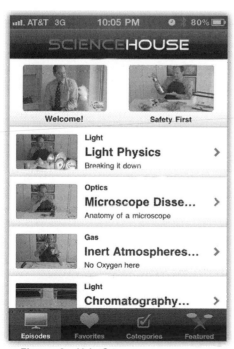

Figure 1—VideoScience

VideoScience is hosted by Dan Menelly, education adviser to the Science House Foundation. Menelly is also a science teacher at the United Nations International School in New York City and a 2010 Albert Einstein Distinguished Educator Fellow, working with the National Science Foundation in the Office of Cyberinfrastructure.

VideoScience is for science teachers, students, and science enthusiasts alike. The experiments and demonstrations are aligned with topics in elementary, middle school, and high school science curricula. When students conduct a science experiment, they need to be able to communicate what they have done. The VideoScience app not only gives teachers and students quick video lessons but also gives students a format to follow when creating their own videos individually or as a group for presentations.

How Does VideoScience Work?

On the iPad, the app can be scrolled through on the left side of the screen. The videos play directly in the app (see Figure 2).

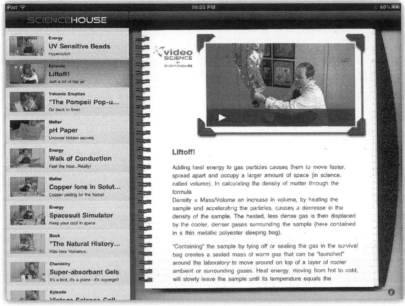

Figure 2—*On-screen video play*

Users can scroll to the very top of the app to use the search window. With the iPad 2, videos will play through VGA out. The iPod Touch and the iPhone allow users to create a favorites menu and scroll through the videos by category (see Figure 3).

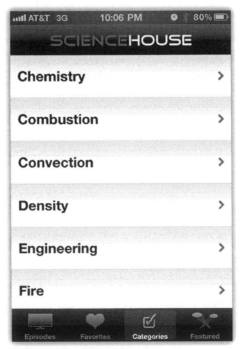

Figure 3—*Videos by category*

If users find a video they want to share, they can forward it to others (see Figure 4). Tapping on the icon on the top right corner of the iPod Touch or iPhone screen, users can view all of the text that goes with the app, including experiment information and items needed to conduct the experiment. On the iPad, the text and the video are both on the right side of the screen. VideoScience offers concept notes, links to purchase the materials needed for experiments, and a blog where users can share their experiences and ask questions.

Figure 4—*Sharing video*

How Can VideoScience Be Used in the Classroom?

Having videos that answer the "whys" in science are always a plus in the classroom. In researching how videos help in science, we were pleasantly surprised to find that short videos used in the class may contribute to a rise in science test scores. One science textbook company has a series of 12 to 15 science videos for the classroom.

When studying friction and forces, for example, the Hovercraft video is a one-minute video that can grab students' interest. There is also a motion video called "Bubble Racing" that can be used in physics or forensic classes. This video introduces solving for an unknown element. If teachers are looking for videos for students on chemical changes in matter, there are several to choose from inside the app.

Ever wondered how light travels in fiber optics cables when they are bent? Check out the motion video "Neon Waterfall." The links to the products needed for this experiment are easy to find and optional items are mentioned in the video. VideoScience is a great asset for the classroom, the homeschooling parent, and students with science fair projects.

World Factbook

App name: World Factbook

Subject areas: Geography, reference

Available for: iPad / iPod Touch / iPhone

Cost: $1.99 for iPad / $0.99 for iPod Touch and iPhone

Requirements: Requires iOS 3.0 or later.

iTunes URL: http://itunes.apple.com/us/app/2011-world-factbook/id307337503?mt=8

Developer web site: http://www.fuzzypeachsoftware.com/

Internet required: No

What Is World Factbook?

World Factbook contains historic and current information for more than 250 countries. There are nine categories of content for each country. These areas include an introduction to the country that highlights major events and current issues and may include a statement about one or two key future trends. Other areas include geography, people, government, economy, communications, transportation, military, and transnational issues. The World Factbook is updated every two weeks.

How Does World Factbook Work?

When the app is opened, the first screen lists world locations on the left, shown in Figure 1.

Figure 1—Opening screen

The first choice is World Data. Countries are listed in alphabetical order under World. On the right side of the screen, users can scroll through the nine categories mentioned above or tap on any of the icons under the word World. There is also an icon in each category explaining the category. In Figure 2, you can see what the background category covers.

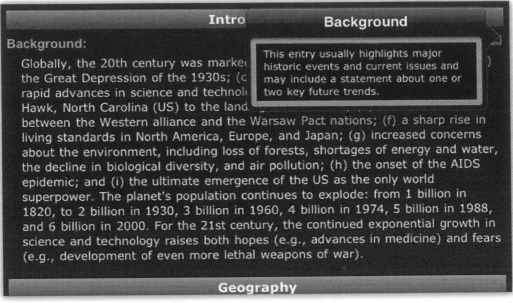

Figure 2—*Background information*

In many of the categories there are graph icons to click on. The graph shows the world rank of the country in that category. In Figure 3, you can see that American Samoa ranks 214th in area.

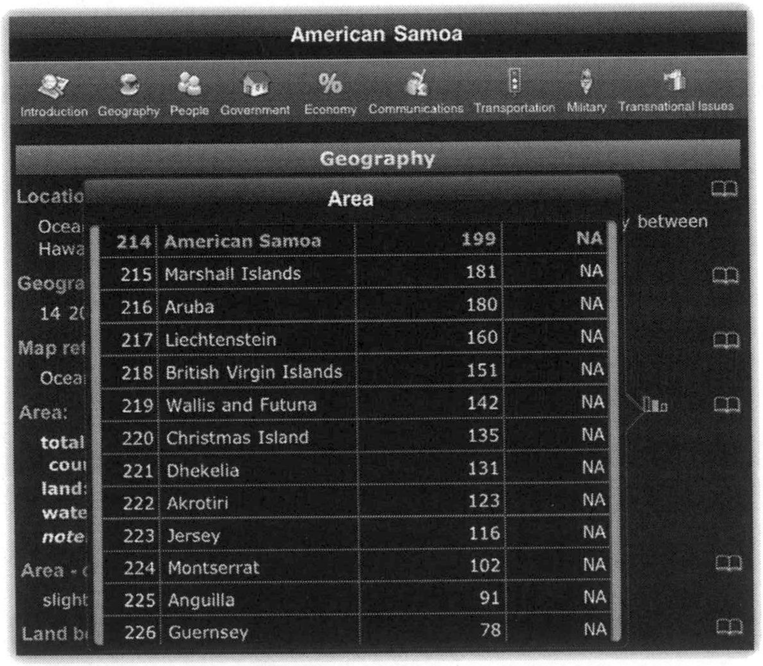

Figure 3—*Ranking list sample*

On the bottom left corner of the app are three tabs. The first one, Locations, is selected when the app is opened. The other two choices are Maps and Comparisons. In Figure 4, whch shows the Maps tab, there are 12 world maps listed.

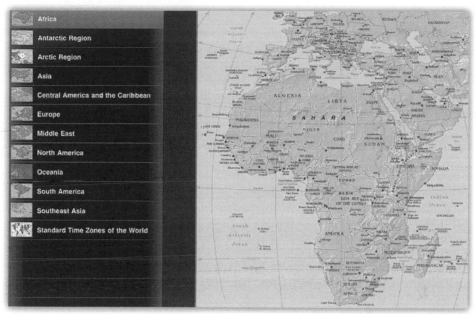

Figure 4—World map listings

In the Comparisons tab (Figure 5), each country is ranked in each of the nine categories listed when the app is opened. The Comparisons tab also breaks down each category.

Country Comparisons	(sq km)	Date
Geography	17,098,242	NA
Area	9,984,670	NA
People	9,826,675	NA
Population	9,596,961	NA
Population growth rate	8,514,877	NA
Birth rate	7,741,220	NA
Death rate	3,287,263	NA
Net migration rate	2,780,400	NA
Infant mortality rate	2,724,900	NA
Life expectancy at birth	2,505,813	NA
	2,381,741	NA
Total fertility rate	2,344,858	NA
HIV/AIDS - adult prevalence rate	2,166,086	NA
HIV/AIDS - people living with HIV/AIDS	2,149,690	NA
HIV/AIDS - deaths	1,964,375	NA
Education expenditures	1,904,569	NA
	1,759,540	NA
Economy	1,648,195	NA
GDP (purchasing power parity)	1,564,116	NA
GDP real growth rate	1,285,216	NA
	1,284,000	NA
	1,267,000	NA
	1,246,700	NA

Locations   Maps   Comparisons

Figure 5—Country comparisons

The category People is divided into 12 areas. In Figure 6, the close-up on the country of Kiribati reveals that as of 2002 it spent 17.8% of its GDP on education.

iPad 🔋		3:50 PM		40% 🔋
Comparisons		Education expenditures		

Rank	Country	(% of GDP)	Date
1	Kiribati	17.80	2002
2	Cuba	13.60	2008
3	Lesotho	12.40	2008
4	Marshall Islands	12.30	2004
5	Palau	10.30	2002

Figure 6—Education expenditures (first five listed)

The 2011 World Factbook is easy to use, and all of the content is inside the app. The app is updated constantly, so recent data can be found on the countries. At the bottom of each country's information, users can see the last date information was updated. It works off-line, which is really important when users may not have wireless Internet available. When clicking on any country, users can see the location of the country on its continent and the country's flag, as well as a close-up of the country and its national capital. Text can be copied from the app for reports also. The text can also be cited correctly, as seen in Figure 7.

Rank	Country	(years)	Date
1	Monaco	89.78	2010 est.
2	Macau	84.38	2010 est.
3	San Marino	82.95	2010 est.
4	Andorra	82.36	2010 est.
5	Japan	82.17	2010 est.
6	Guernsey	82.08	2010 est.
7	Singapore	82.06	2010 est.
8	Hong Kong	81.96	2010 est.
		81.72	2010 est.
	file://var/mobile/Applications/7FF7F1B0-B4DD-4CDE-835E-530...ationLink/sz.html	81.29	2010 est.
		81.28	2010 est.
	Open	81.09	2010 est.
		81.07	2010 est.
	Copy		
14	Swe...	80.97	2010 est.
15	Switzerland	80.97	2010 est.
16	Israel	80.86	2010 est.
17	Iceland	80.79	2010 est.
18	Anguilla	80.77	2010 est.
19	Bermuda	80.60	2010 est.
20	Cayman Islands	80.57	2010 est.
21	Isle of Man	80.53	2010 est.

Figure 7—Copying text for report use

How Can World Factbook Be Used in the Classroom?

When students need informational text or data about a country, this app gives them a way to quickly and easily find facts. Students can study the role that geography plays on economic development, and they can use the app to categorize and interpret data for ordering complex information about the Earth including climate, political, agricultural, economic, and perceptual information.

When comparing life expectancies between a communist state, Vietnam, and a democratic country, the United States, students will quickly find differencies in life expectancies. With the World Factbook app, students can get an overview of other things that may contribute to these differences, including wars and natural disasters, population density, birth rates, and infant mortality rates. Students can use this app to analyze the relationship between a country's infrastructure and its level of development. The app gives students information they need when challenged to describe how transportation, communication technologies, and even social networking have contributed to cultural merging and political unrest.

Advanced Uses

Using the transnational issues information on the countries, teachers can quickly create discussion around why countries from different parts of the world have interests in foreign affairs sometimes thousands of miles away. Discussions and projects can be created on trading partners of the countries and where imports and exports come from for the countries.

The World Factbook can be used as a factor analysis tool to analyze and isolate the importance of each of the many factors that go into a particular result or outcome. The example in Marc Prensky's book, *Teaching Digital Natives,* is "To what extent is increased life expectancy a result of better nutrition, better healthcare, less smoking, and other factors?" The World Factbook app helps answer many of those questions by individual country. These data pieces are more up-to-date than a textbook, and any of the data can be copied and pasted into a word processing program on the iPad.

These questions can only lead to new questions. For example, would better education lead to better health care or to increased life expectancy? Graphs could be created as a way to use math skills to answer questions; for example, changing percentages to decimals and so forth. Predictions could then be made on the data.

Another social studies question could be "How do civil wars affect population shifts in African countries?" This would be especially interesting since you could also look at how the Civil War affected the United States. In science, students can follow exploratory observations such as "What grows where and when?" or "What are sanctions, how do they work, and how do we know what to sanction?" This app begins answering these questions.

Index

Notes

Notes

21st Century Fluency Project

Also Available in Books and DVDs

Understanding the Digital Generation

Teaching and Learning in the New Digital Landscape

Today's world is different for our children. The technologies we take for granted or simply don't understand have become a part of our children's identities. Explore the characteristics of the new digital generation, and how education can be modified to enhance their learning experiences while supporting both traditional literacy and essential new 21st Century Fluencies. *Also on DVD.*

www.understandingthedigitalgeneration.com

Living on the Future Edge

Windows on Tomorrow

The exponential changes and advances in electronics and online culture that we have witnessed in recent years have been staggering. The very nature of change itself is changing, and it all seems to be happening so rapidly. *Living on the Future Edge* covers 6 exciting exponential trends that are clearing a path to tomorrow where the changes can truly benefit us all. *Also on DVD.*

www.livingonthefutureedge.com

The Digital Diet

Today's Digital Tools in Small Bytes

Understanding the digital world we and our students live in today can be a daunting process for the newcomer. In this book, the authors offer a chance to try an actual "digital diet". Feast on a tantalizing buffet of blogs, wikis, online video, search engines, social networking tools like Facebook, and much more. Sample the delights of each chapter as you dive into the exciting digital world!

www.thedigitaldiet.com

www.fluency21.com

LITERACY

is NOT enough